USING EXPERIENTIAL LEARNING IN THE CLASSROOM

Practical Ideas for All Educators

Scott D. Wurdinger

ScarecrowEducation
Lanham, Maryland • Toronto • Oxford
2005

Published in the United States of America
by ScarecrowEducation
An imprint of The Rowman & Littlefield Publishing Group, Inc.
4501 Forbes Boulevard, Suite 200, Lanham, Maryland 20706
www.scaroweducation.com

PO Box 317
Oxford
OX2 9RU, UK

British Library Cataloguing in Publication Information Available

Library of Congress Cataloging-in-Publication Data

Wurdinger, Scott D.
  Using experiential learning in the classroom : practical ideas for all
educators / Scott D. Wurdinger.
     p. cm.
  Includes bibliographical references.
  ISBN 1-57886-240-X (pbk. : alk. paper)
  1. Active learning. 2. Experiential learning. I. Title.

LB1027.23.W87 2005
371.39—dc22   2004027836

Manufactured in the United States of America.

To my mentors, who helped shape my thinking over the years: Dr. Galen Eiben of Wartburg College in Waverly, Iowa; Sigurd Olson of Ely Junior College in Ely, Minnesota; Dr. Roger Knutson and Dr. Kent Finanger of Luther College in Decorah, Iowa; Dr. Jasper Hunt of Minnesota State University in Mankato; Dr. Bruce Jacobs of Ferris State University in Big Rapids, Michigan; Jeff Boeke, director of Adventure Based Experiential Educators in Oconomowoc, Wisconsin; and David Lockett, principal of Jefferson Elementary School in Stevens Point, Wisconsin.

CONTENTS

PREFACE

The idea to write a book on the topic of experiential learning evolved from the many discussions I had with a retired dean of continuing education named Bruce Jacobs. He and I would sit around his outdoor fire pit at night and discuss problems with teaching in higher education and high school, and potential solutions for improving learning in the classroom. He did not have an academic background in experiential learning but was himself an experiential learner who used this process with his students, colleagues, and children.

During our discussions he would gently probe by asking questions that would grow with intensity as the discussion progressed. I remember in one of our last discussions, not long before his passing, he asked me why I wanted to write this book. "What value will this book hold, and do you think your words will really make a difference in the way educators teach their classes?" he asked. He was pushing me to define the premise of this book in a sentence or two. These discussions helped me focus and clarify the need for educators to change from a lecture-driven format to an experiential format. Bruce motivated me to write this book, just as he motivated many others to excel beyond their preconceived limitations. It is largely due to his influence that I have written this book.

This book provides educators with useful ideas and resources on how to implement experiential learning in their classrooms. However, in order to avoid some of the problems from past attempts to implement experiential learning, it is important to first understand what it is and why it is effective. Once educators understand the theory behind the practice, they can begin to more easily implement experiential learning into their classrooms. Implementing the process, however, requires time and effort. Experiential learning is not as simple as the information assimilation process, where educators give lectures, tests, and then a grade. Implementing experiential learning requires educators to think of projects, activities, and field experiences that promote problem solving in their classrooms. It requires more time for students to think their way through problems because several trial-and-error attempts might be necessary in order to find solutions. Implementing experiential learning also requires creativity and effort on the educator's part, to design curriculums that incorporate activities, projects, and field experiences.

The first part of this book focuses on the theory of experiential learning. Chapters one, two, and three are theoretical in nature and discuss the definitions, theory, and effectiveness of experiential learning. A theoretical foundation, as well as an understanding of the potential benefits, provides readers with information that will help make it easier for individuals to apply theory.

Chapters four, five, and six provide readers with examples of implementing experiential learning in specific schools and classrooms. Chapter four explains how four different high schools have taken this process and integrated it throughout their entire curriculums. Although their school philosophies differ somewhat, the principles that undergird the experiential learning process are common to all four schools. Examples of activities, projects, and field experiences from these schools are threaded throughout the chapter.

Chapter five explains how educators can use this process in their own classrooms. Examples from high school and college educators are sprinkled throughout the chapter, as well as explanations on how to include activities, projects, and field experiences in classroom courses. Chapters five and six both provide readers with tools and resources they might wish to explore for future use. The examples from these two chapters will allow educators to create their own experiential curriculums.

Chapter six provides educators with ideas about how to assess experiential learning in the classroom. How to use performance-based assessment tools such as rubrics, self-assessments, constructed response exercises, and portfolios is discussed, and examples of each are provided so that educators can duplicate the forms for their own use. An explanation behind why educators should use performance-based as opposed to standards-based assessments is also given.

Finally, chapter seven discusses several barriers that educators may face when attempting to implement experiential learning, as well as ways to overcome them. This chapter will, hopefully, prevent educators from becoming frustrated with the process and help them find ways to incorporate experiential learning into all their classes.

If one agrees with the motto "Experience is the best teacher," then I have had an excellent teacher over the past 20 years. During these years I have taught high school, undergraduate, and graduate students, so many of the examples mentioned in this book come from my experiences working with these students. It is my hope that high school and college level educators are able to take the ideas contained in this book and transform their classrooms into more dynamic learning environments where students are excited to come to class because they enjoy the learning process.

ACKNOWLEDGMENTS

I would like to thank my family, Annette, Madeline, and Lauren, for allowing me the time to work on this project. They have always been supportive and understanding of my work. Annette would usually drive on vacation trips so that I could tap away on my laptop—thanks for driving!

Jasper Hunt has provided me with unconditional support over the past 20 years. He served as my graduate advisor while I was working on a master's degree in experiential education, as well as an adjunct faculty member on my doctoral committee. Today I am lucky to be his colleague in the Department of Educational Leadership, with an office directly next to his. He ignited a fire in me to pursue my passion with experiential learning and over the years has had an enormous impact on my thinking. I am deeply indebted to him for helping me become a more effective educator and writer. I would also like to thank Julie Carlson, another faculty member in the experiential education graduate program, for providing a thorough critique of the book. Julie also provided important information in the assessment chapter by creating and refining learning contracts, assessment plans and reports, and rubrics used in the program.

Michael Miller, dean of the College of Education at Minnesota State University, Mankato, deserves a special thank you for approving my application for course releases, which provided me with valuable writing time.

Ron Newell, codirector of Edvisions, provided wonderful ideas on how to improve the book. His book *Passion for Learning* has inspired me to incorporate more project-based learning in my own courses.

Pete Allison, editor of the *Journal of Adventure Education and Outdoor Learning* and professor at the University of Edinburgh, provided valuable feedback on grammar and content. His editorial skills are superb, and he let me know it.

Maureen Prenn and Jean Haar from Minnesota State University, Mankato, gave me some wonderful feedback on how to be more accurate in assessing experiential education courses, as well as assessing the process of experiential learning.

Kellian Clink, research librarian from Minnesota State University, Mankato, provided a variety of bibliographic material while I was recuperating from back surgery. Her generous support allowed me to collect important information for the book.

I would like to thank the Minnesota State University, Mankato, dispositions task force (Darrol Bussler, Heidi Pellett, Patricia Hoffman, Dottie Engen-Barker, Maureen Prenn, and Andy Johnson), who helped create a dispositions form for the College of Education, using the framework from Charlotte Danielson's *Enhancing Student Achievement: A Framework for School Improvement* (2002).

David Lockett, a principal in Stevens Point, Wisconsin, provided numerous discussions and ideas about the theory and practice of experiential learning and how to make my ideas useful to high school teachers. Ramona Lundberg, a high school science teacher in Clear Lake, South Dakota, also provided ideas on how to make the book more user friendly for teachers. Their ideas helped me tremendously.

Robert Hugg and Marin Burton, experiential education graduate students, provided valuable ideas on how to make the book more useful for college students.

Ilene Shimota, director of experiential learning at St. Olaf College, provided enthusiastic support for the book in its earlier stage.

Finally, Diane Siebert, administrative assistant in the Department of Educational Leadership, provided feedback on the overall mechanics of the book. I am sincerely grateful for all her help on this project.

CHANGING TEACHING FORMATS

I remember sitting in one of my high school classes over 30 years ago, listening to the teacher lecture about various milestones in U.S. history. He would usually talk for the first half of class and then hand out a worksheet, which was to be completed during the second half of class. Most of my classes consisted of a similar format: taking notes, filling out worksheets, and taking quizzes and tests, all for the purpose of determining whether I was smart enough to go on to college. Time went by slowly. I watched the clock constantly, waiting for the bell to ring so I could do it all over again the following period. How would I ever make it through four years of college if classes were going to consist of the same boring format? Fortunately, I developed a strong interest in wildlife biology my senior year of high school, which in spite of all the boring lectures I experienced, provided a strong enough impetus for me to enroll in college.

My interest in wildlife biology carried me through to the end of college; however, it was several lengthy experiences in the field that fueled my desire to complete my undergraduate degree. I knew I needed the degree to obtain a decent job. I would attend classes for a year, getting extremely frustrated listening to lectures and cramming for tests, so I would take the following year off to experience life. During these reprieves from college I helped conduct research on timber wolves for the

U.S. Fish and Wildlife Service, conducted research on beavers for the U.S. Forest Service, worked as an instructor for Outward Bound in northern Minnesota, and went on numerous mountaineering and canoeing expeditions. These direct experiences were much more meaningful than sitting listening to professors lecture about information found in textbooks and about their own past experiences.

Unfortunately, it seems that not much has changed in the classroom over the past three decades. In one study, Courts and McInerny (1993) discovered that the most common concern students had about the instruction they were receiving was the overreliance on lecture and workbook exercises. What students wanted was more interaction and more "hands-on learning" (pp. 33–38). Levine and Cureton's (1998) comprehensive study on college students also discovered that educators continue to prefer abstract ideas and passive methods of learning, whereas students prefer active methods of learning. However, extensive research studies, such as the ones just mentioned, are not necessary to determine whether teachers are still lecturing and handing out worksheets. All one has to do is ask students what they are experiencing in the classroom or walk through the halls past high school and college classrooms to realize that lecture continues to be the dominant teaching format.

I continue to wonder why educators haven't incorporated more experiential learning into their classrooms. We know all students don't like to sit passively taking notes to be memorized for the next exam. Nobody does! Currently the No Child Left Behind legislation is calling for even more testing. "The explosion in testing, particularly high stakes testing, over the past two decades has put enormous weight on tests and has placed them squarely in the center of schooling" (Rothman, 2001, p. 431). High schools, colleges, and universities continue to use paper and pencil tests as the primary tool to measure intelligence. Students are inundated with tests, which unfortunately promotes the use of lecture as the primary teaching method, resulting in a learning process based primarily on memorization. The dichotomy between how students learn best and how educators teach is not new. Dewey mentioned this idea as early as 1916 when he stated, "Formal instruction, on the contrary, easily becomes remote and dead— abstract and bookish, to use the ordinary words of depreciation" (p. 8).

It appears that tests and more passive methods of learning will continue for at least the next several years because "the new legislation, reauthorizing the Elementary and Secondary Education Act (ESEA), will tie federal education funding to improvements in student test scores" (Heinecke, Curry-Corcoran, & Moon, 2003, p. 7). Schools that do not meet specific standards run the risk of losing federal funding, which will most likely result in a situation where educators spend much of their time "teaching to the tests." Outside of school we live by the motto "Experience is the best teacher," but in school a different motto is promoted, "Memorizing information is the best teacher."

It is time for traditional education to change the way it views knowledge. Traditional education, which consists of compartmentalized subject matter and short class periods, relies heavily on lecture and memorization. Knowledge should not be defined as one's ability to retain large amounts of information or receive high scores on tests, such as the ACT, SAT, PPST, GRE, MCAT, LSAT, or the myriad of others students are required to take.

According to the Secretary's Commission on Achieving Necessary Skills (SCANS) report, schools should focus on teaching "basic literacy and computational skills, thinking skills necessary to put knowledge to work, and personal qualities such as dedication and trustworthiness" because these are the skills needed to be a productive member in the work environment (2001, p. 72). Individuals need to know how to solve real-life problems and how to be team players. The world demands that people have the ability to solve problems and get along with one another, which means educators need to change their view of knowledge and focus on teaching these life skills.

There is hope for change coming from reports written by other national organizations as well. The National Association of Secondary School Principals (NASSP) wrote a report in 1996 titled *Breaking Ranks: Changing an American Institution*, which was recently rewritten and is now titled *Breaking Ranks II: Strategies for Leading High School Reform* (2004). This report provides a wonderful set of recommendations for reforming American high schools. The following is a sample of some of the recommendations that support the use of experiential learning:

Each student will have a Personal Plan for Progress that will be reviewed often to ensure that the high school takes individual needs into consideration and to allow students, within reasonable parameters, to design their own methods for learning in an effort to meet high standards.

Every high school student will have a Personal Adult Advocate to help him or her personalize the educational experience.

Teachers will convey a sense of caring to their students so that their students feel that their teachers share a stake in their learning.

The high school will reorganize the traditional department structure in order to integrate the school's curriculum to the extent possible and emphasize depth over breadth of coverage.

The content of the curriculum, where practical, should connect to real-life applications of knowledge and skills to help students link their education to the future.

The high school will promote service programs and student activities as integral to an education, providing opportunities for all students that support and extend academic learning.

The academic program will extend beyond the high school campus to take advantage of learning opportunities outside the four walls of the building

Teachers will design high quality work and teach in ways that engage students, encourage them to persist, and, when the work is successfully completed, result in student satisfaction and their acquisition of knowledge, critical thinking and problem solving skills, and other abilities valued by society.

Teachers will be adept at acting as coaches and as facilitators of learning to promote more active involvement of students in their own learning (NASSP, 2004, p. 18).

These recommendations, as you will read later in chapter three, are directly tied to some of the key underlying principles of experiential learning. It is obvious when educators and administrators develop such recommendations, as well as make statements such as "The old ways that no longer work must yield to change" (NASSP, 1996, p. 2), that the status quo must be challenged with more progressive educational philosophies such as experiential learning.

The primary purpose of this book is to challenge educators to use more experiential learning in their classrooms. Although passive forms of education occur at all grade levels, this book focuses on high school and higher education environments where lecture appears to be the most prevalent teaching format. Educators at these grade levels should integrate projects, activities, and field-based experiences into their curriculums so that students are engaged in solving real-life problems.

For educators who use lecture as their primary teaching format, it means changing teaching formats to include more active methods of learning. It means changing from a completely content-driven curriculum to one that includes more process. It means helping students identify relevant problems, develop plans to solve these problems, test out these plans against reality, and eventually reflect on what they learned. Rather than beginning the learning process with information to be memorized, it means helping students identify interesting problems that will engage them on an emotional and intellectual level.

If traditional education doesn't begin to use more experiential learning, it will lose its students. In the state of Minnesota alone, over 86,000 K–12 students sought out alternative schooling in 2003–2004 through alternative schools, charter schools, home schooling, and others (education.state.mn.us/html/intro_data_student_data.htm). Students are naturally curious and want to learn, but educators need to provide them with a more engaging learning process than what is currently being used.

My wife asked me, "Why are you writing this book? What are you going to say that has not already been said about experiential learning?" My response was, "I want to write the book to convince educators that experiential learning should be the primary teaching format used in the classroom because it utilizes a dynamic approach to knowledge where students solve problems and apply information, which in turn motivates them to learn."

Time and again students in my Philosophy of Experiential Education graduate course, which consists of a variety of educators from different disciplines, mention at the end of the course that they believe in the philosophy of experiential learning, but it is impractical and extremely difficult to implement in our current education system. My response back is usually something like, "But you now realize that it is a more effective learning process, so why wouldn't you at least attempt to implement it?"

The time has come to change the way many educators view knowledge. Students need to be active learners and solve problems. Many are bored with lecture and other teaching formats that result in passive learning. They do not want to sit and listen to someone talk for entire class periods. Society requires individuals to be active learners that are able to solve problems, so our schools should mirror what society expects of its citizenry.

This book is not about how to create large-scale systemic change. It is about how to implement experiential learning in classroom settings. It is about how to use experiential learning within the existing system. Educators sometimes think they need to scrap the current educational system in order to utilize experiential learning formats, and in some cases, such as the four school reform movements discussed in chapter four, educators have created new systems in order to hold true to their educational beliefs. Even though these schools have been extremely successful, they are not where the majority of educators work. The majority of educators work in traditional school settings.

That is why organizations such as NASSP have created recommendations for change that "draw strength and authority from the fact that it arises from the inside and does not descend on high schools from the outside" (1996, p. 1). Recommendations coming from public school administrators and teachers, as opposed to academic consultants or legislators, provide greater validity, support, and encouragement for those educators aspiring to use more experiential learning in their classrooms. This book was written for those educators.

2

WHAT IS EXPERIENTIAL LEARNING?

Scholars, particularly in the fields of outdoor education, service learning, and adult education, have written extensively about experiential learning theories and their applications to these learning environments. In the field of outdoor education, for example, experiential learning models have been developed to help educators maximize student learning in outdoor settings (Bunting & Townley, 1999; Wurdinger & Priest, 1999). Likewise, scholarship from the field of adult education suggests students gain more from direct experiences as opposed to more traditional approaches to education (Boud, Cohen, & Walker, 1993; Warner-Weil & McGill, 1989). The service-learning field echoes much of the literature in adult education and provides examples of how to integrate experiential learning into higher education curriculums (Eyler & Giles, 1999; Stanton, Giles, & Cruz, 1999; Rhoades & Howard, 1998; Jacoby & Associates, 1996). Individual scholars continue to create and refine experiential learning models in attempts to improve education, but national organizations have also spent considerable time creating definitions for the same reason.

The Association for Experiential Education (AEE) defines experiential learning as "a process through which a learner constructs knowledge, skill, and value from direct experience" (www.aee.org/ndef/html). The National

Society for Experiential Education (NSEE) defines it as "inductive, beginning with raw experience that is processed through an intentional learning format and transformed into working, useable knowledge" (www.nsee.org). Many of the models created by scholars in different fields are aligned with these two definitions, suggesting that experiential learning is a reactive process in which learning occurs by reflecting on previous experiences. In other words, we experience something and learn from it only if we reflect upon it afterward. This in turn implies that if educators wish to use this learning process, they need to provide students with experiences and then help them reflect upon them so that learning occurs.

This approach to learning provides educators with a general understanding of experiential learning but does not provide them with a practical approach to designing and implementing this type of learning in their classroom environments. Dewey (1973), however, did define a specific learning sequence with a starting and end point that allows educators to be proactive and design lessons that incorporate experiential learning. His theory helps ensure that thinking occurs not only after an experience but also throughout the entire process.

Dewey spent the better part of his life researching and writing about the value of experience in the learning process. He was a true experiential educator, creating a lab school at the University of Chicago in order "to work out in the concrete, instead of merely in the head or on paper, a theory of the unity of knowledge" (1936, p. 204). Creating the lab school allowed him to observe students and test out his theories firsthand about learning and teaching.

After years of experimentation, Dewey identified several key components of his learning theory, which he called the "pattern of inquiry" (1973, p. 223). Inquiry is initiated with a problem that perplexes the student and is followed by observing the variables associated with the problem, developing a plan, testing this plan against reality to discover a solution, and reflecting on the results to determine whether there are other or better solutions to the problem. The testing phase requires the learner to apply information, which is often left out of the learning that occurs in traditional education settings. Application is the critical component that identifies his theory as experiential and provides educators with a framework for designing learning activities where students combine thinking with doing.

Working through his learning process from beginning to end, however, requires time and work from both educators and students. Solving a problem may take several class periods or the better part of a semester, depending upon the difficulty of the problem. It requires work from students because they may have to go through numerous trial-and-error episodes before finding a solution. Students learn from making mistakes; however, they must be provided with an environment that allows them to learn from mistakes.

Many school environments penalize students for making mistakes. Exams and tests often promote competition, which may lead to a fear of failure. To stay clear of such situations, Martin-Kniep (2000) suggests promoting an environment where students "feel safe about sharing what they think. This condition is present when teachers make a habit of celebrating mistakes and reminding students that mistakes generate true opportunities for learning" (p. 76). Allowing students to make mistakes may also lead to a situation where they retain more information because it is a more challenging learning process.

The sequence of Dewey's experiential learning process is critical and should begin with a problem or challenge that has some relevancy to the student's life. For example, my 13-year-old daughter has little interest in figuring out percentages on math worksheets; however, when taken on shopping outings she becomes extremely interested in figuring out percentages and how much particular sale items cost. When the problem has relevancy she becomes focused and begins observing certain variables such as how much money she has, how much different items cost, what she really needs as opposed to what she wants, and the quality of the clothing she is interested in purchasing. She makes a plan on what items to purchase according to these different variables, then tests her plan by purchasing and wearing the clothes. Finally, she reflects on the experience by determining whether her money was well spent.

When interest is initiated, the learning sequence outlined by Dewey often occurs without much assistance from the educator. The key is to find out what students are interested in so that appropriate problems can be identified. The educator's role is to guide the student through this learning process and provide information and resources when students get stuck.

I observe this problem-solving process in several of my experiential education courses. Two in particular are designed specifically as project-based courses where students plan, design, and implement their projects over the course of a semester. Developing new curriculum and using new teaching techniques are common projects in these courses. Since many of the students are professional educators, these courses provide them with opportunities to explore new ideas and develop new ways of doing things in their classrooms. Planning, designing, and implementing these new ideas require them to use the pattern of inquiry and think their way through the process. Students in these courses often realize at the conclusion of their projects that this approach to learning is beneficial for them, and so they often begin utilizing this process with their students. Project-based education is an effective tool for engaging students in Dewey's pattern of inquiry.

Another definition of experiential learning, which is different from Dewey's but useful in this discussion, suggests that experiential learning occurs outside traditional classroom settings. "Experiential learning is a broad spectrum of educational experiences, such as community service, field work, sensitivity training groups, internships, cooperative education involving work in business or industry, and undergraduate participation in faculty research" (McKeachie, 1999, p. 154). This definition focuses on real-life experiences that occur outside the walls of a classroom, where students engage in a variety of learning experiences.

Not all out-of-class experiences result in learning or incorporate Dewey's pattern of inquiry. Problem solving is often required during such experiences, but not always. When students do not understand why they are involved or do not reflect on the experience, it may lead to a noneducative experience (Dewey, 1938).

For instance, if students do not understand the purpose behind a service project (such as building a wing dam to control stream erosion), they may not learn anything from the experience. They might even resent the experience and the people associated with it, especially since hard labor is required to complete the project. Leading questions such as the following can initiate interest in solving the problem: Why should the class build this dam? What will happen to the stream environment if the dam is not built? What will be the rate of erosion? What will eventually happen to the house that sits next to the stream? Where should the dam be built? What material should be used to build the wing dam?

Once students understand the importance of building the dam, they can begin researching and exploring wing dams. They can develop a plan based on their findings and then test their findings by building the dam. They can return to the site after a period of time to determine if the dam is working. If it is not, they can develop a new plan and rebuild the dam until they are successful.

Meaning and interest may be lost if the educator takes charge and tells students what to do to complete the project. When this happens, students are doing something, but they are not engaged in the problem-solving process. They are reproducing what the educator tells them to do, which limits the amount of problem solving required of students. This is what Cohen (1986) refers to as direct instruction, which is telling students what to do and how to do it. In her comprehensive book on group work, she says it is critical to delegate authority because "it makes students responsible for their work" and "free to accomplish their task in the way they think best" (p. 2). Educators must allow students to take responsibility for their work, as well as intentionally include Dewey's pattern of inquiry in out-of-class experiences, so that learning occurs.

Field experiences, such as the ones McKeachie mentions in his definition of experiential learning, can provide students with valuable information about their interests and career goals. Students can explore various occupations through these field experiences to determine whether they wish to pursue them on a long-term basis. But, it is important for educators who oversee such experiences to incorporate the pattern of inquiry so that students are thinking and solving problems while involved in these experiences. This will solidify the process of experiential learning, as opposed to promoting blind experiences that lack any learning.

The pattern of inquiry (which is a learning theory) and field-based experiences (which occur outside the classroom) are two common views of experiential learning. Another common view of experiential learning centers on classroom-based approaches, such as cooperative learning, collaborative learning, project-based learning, and problem-based learning. These approaches incorporate problem solving and hands-on learning in classroom settings. All may include group interaction; however, project-based learning may be completed by students independently of one another. These classroom approaches to teaching have similarities in that students are at the center of the learning process, taking active roles creating, presenting, and discussing ideas that require them to solve problems. One key idea behind all these approaches is to begin the learning process with a problem that leads to interaction, such as discussion or hands-on involvement, and can be used as a mechanism to engage students in a variety of activities or projects.

Projects and activities, which are associated more with the classroom approaches just mentioned, and field-based experiences that incorporate Dewey's pattern of inquiry, are three tools used to define experiential learning in this book. In attempts to define these tools, educators should keep in mind that definitions for the three tools are less important than understanding how to incorporate the pattern of inquiry with each tool. These three tools typically require hands-on participation and interaction with other individuals in order to complete the learning process. Students may also need to leave the classroom and venture out into the world, as mentioned by McKeachie, in order to discover answers to various problems.

Of the three tools, activities have the greatest potential to be misinterpreted. An activity is not taking a paper and pencil test, filling out a worksheet, or answering questions about a reading assignment. Henry (1989) categorizes different definitions of experiential learning—one describes activity-based learning as including "practicals, simulations, games, role plays or expressive approaches like drama, art, and imaginative activities" (p. 32). An activity may be viewed as being more educator directed; however, the focus should be on solving problems through hands-on involvement.

Activities may be group oriented and focus on things such as identifying common goals. For instance, in my Organization and Systems Change course, I use an activity where each student identifies a potential problem or question he or she would like to explore as a project and writes it down on a sticky sheet. In small groups of two or three, students place their sticky sheets on the classroom walls. In the process of doing this, they look for similar themes and cluster their ideas next to one another on the walls. Once themes have been identified, students walk to their sticky sheets and discuss with others in their groups whether they would like to work with others who have similar project ideas. This activity is the starting point for the pattern of inquiry because students have identified relevant problems they would like to solve.

Activities might also focus on developing group cohesiveness. For instance, student interviews, where students partner up and ask one another a variety of questions in order to introduce each other to the rest of the class, allow students to get to know one another better. The interviews also engage them in the pattern of inquiry. The problem is to get to know your partner well enough to introduce him or her to the rest of the class. The planning phase requires asking questions and taking notes. The testing phase is the introduction itself, and afterward one might reflect on whether or not enough details were provided to adequately introduce the person.

Educators should remember, however, that such activities should help students determine how they might use such skills for future learning. For instance, a student may develop an interest in journalism after participating in a series of interview activities. This could lead the student to seek out field-based experiences such as attending conferences and workshops on journalism techniques or doing an internship with a professional news reporter working in the field. It could also lead to a project such as designing and creating a manual covering the ethics of news reporting.

An activity can be a discussion about a book that attempts to uncover the author's meaning, or it could involve doing some type of aerobic exercise to determine maximum heart rate or calorie output. Activities can be just about anything that requires solving a problem that is relevant to the student's life.

Projects will be defined as things students create, build, or produce themselves. Gardner (1991) is highly in favor of the project method over more traditional methods: "In the course of their careers in the American schools of today, most students take hundreds, if not thousands, of tests. They develop skill to a highly calibrated degree in an exercise that will essentially become useless immediately after their last day in school. In contrast, when one examines life outside of school, projects emerge as pervasive" (p. 216). Projects are more meaningful than tests because students must think, plan, and execute their ideas to produce something from their own creativity.

The amount of time required to complete a project depends on its complexity. Problems will arise from the projects themselves. For instance, projects such as writing portfolios and manuals, developing programs and curriculum, creating games and activities, and designing web pages require students to develop plans, research different ideas, try things out, and solve numerous problems before the project is completed.

Students at the graduate school level are often interested in developing projects they will use at their workplace, so motivation is usually not an issue. High school and undergraduate students may require more guidance during the project process. It is important to guide them through the process so they do not get stuck and give up on the project. Knoll's (1997) exhaustive study on the "project method" notes that Dewey was in disagreement with Kilpatrick (one of Dewey's students and friends) about how much guidance educators should provide to their students.

> Dewey's primary objection was the one-sided orientation on the child. In his view, pupils by themselves were incapable of planning projects and activities—they needed the aid of a teacher who would ensure the continuous process of learning and growth. To Dewey, the "project" was not (as it was to Kilpatrick) to be an "enterprise of the child," but rather a "common enterprise" of teachers and pupils. (p. 5)

The educator's role is to help students identify an appropriate project and, once students begin work, help them find the necessary information that will move them forward in the discovery process. Self-assessment could be a valuable tool that provides students with focus over the length of the project.

Field-based experiences are defined as those experiences that involve working directly with a professional in the field. In undergraduate and graduate education, these types of experiences are often referred to as field experiences, observations, practicums, internships, and so on. Examples include working with a local business professional to understand how a small business operates, banding ducks with a conservation officer to determine migration patterns, or working with a teacher to learn the skills of teaching. Once again problems will arise naturally from working in the field. For instance, what are the best accounting practices? How does one capture a duck without harming its wings? What are the most effective delivery methods for teaching? These are all questions that may crop up while involved in such field experiences.

A problem or question must be intertwined with activities, projects, and field-based experiences. This will help ensure that a combination of thinking and doing occurs in the learning process. Activities and projects usually require less time to complete than a field-based experience. For instance, a project such as building a wooden duck box will take less time than a field-based experience working with a carpenter. Building a wooden duck box might take a couple of hours; learning carpentry skills could take years.

With all three tools, students need to understand what problems or questions they are attempting to answer before pursuing them. The educator's role, or in some situations the professional's role, is to help students identify and clarify problems and questions so that when students begin the problem-solving process they are headed in the right direction at the outset.

LESSONS FROM THE PAST

An important lesson from the past that relates directly to the previous section is to understand the theory behind experiential learning before attempting to implement it in the classroom. The theory of experiential learning was misinterpreted in the past, which may have been the primary reason why most of the lab schools modeled after Dewey's lab school closed their doors. Lab schools cropped up all over the United States between 1930 and 1950 and began incorporating hands-on experiences and activities into their curriculums (Van Til, 1969, p.12). The problem with many of these schools was that students were experiencing things but not necessarily learning from their experiences. Educators thought that as long as they were providing students with hands-on experiences, learning would follow.

This, however, was not Dewey's original intention when he developed the pattern of inquiry. He even mentions that all experiences are not necessarily educative and that teachers need to guide students along the process so that they seek answers to relevant problems (1938, p. 25).

Minnesota State University, Mankato (MSU, Mankato), where I teach, once had a lab school that utilized an experience-based approach to education. After reviewing several videotapes of the school in action, I am not convinced that teachers understood Dewey's philosophy. The lab school was obviously dedicated to an experiential approach, but it appeared that purpose and reflection may have been lacking in the educational process.

Another factor that may have caused problems for lab schools was perception. Lab schools appeared to be extremely chaotic, with a lack of control by teachers. In some cases this may have held true, but in others students were focused on what they were doing but were not tied to their chairs and could move around at will to pursue their learning. This situation appeared as if students had too much freedom and were not capable of being self-directed with their learning experiences.

Method of assessment may have also presented a problem for lab schools. Van Til (1969) notes that lab schools were excellent at providing "a different type of learning incorporating block time, solving cross-disciplinary problems, creative writing, and social travel" (p. 12). These types of learning experiences are difficult to assess with a paper and pencil test. So, students asked to take standardized tests probably did not fare well, but when asked to apply information probably did exceptionally well. This situation may have led to the perception that lab school students were not learning anything.

The key to combating these issues today is to focus on the pattern of inquiry when engaging students in activities, projects, and field-based experiences. Educators should make sure students understand why they are doing what they are doing before doing it. Allow time for students to verbalize why and what they are doing. Setting aside time for students to express their questions and ideas helps solidify their understanding of the questions and problems associated with activities, projects, and field-based experiences. If students are engaged in longer-term projects and activities, provide time for daily meetings so students can ask questions in order to stay focused. The next chapter not only explains why experiential learning is a highly effective learning process but also suggests that educators should be implementing this process because it mirrors what is expected of individuals in reality.

WHY EXPERIENTIAL
LEARNING WORKS

The reasons why experiential learning is effective are intricately woven together. At the very outset of this learning process, freedom—or at least the perception of freedom—must be provided so that students can choose a topic of their interest. This does not mean total freedom to choose whatever they like. Public school teachers, for instance, are obligated to cover certain topics within their subject areas, but they can provide students with choices on how and when they cover the material. Even graduate students, who are often very self-directed, are obligated to use prescribed methods for doing research. Their research topics may be expanded or narrowed depending upon the complexity of the problem. Freedom, along with some guidance when necessary, allows students to voice ideas on what it is they wish to study and how to study it. Freedom empowers students to take control of their learning, thereby promoting greater intrinsic motivation. It allows students to tap into their own interests, choose relevant problems, search for solutions, and discover knowledge that is useful for their future learning.

STUDENT INTEREST

Student interest is critical to the learning process. When interest is lacking, learning may quickly go awry. Dewey (1916) argues that learning will not occur at all in such situations. Educators may try to force students to learn by threatening them with quizzes and tests, or they might try to "sugarcoat" a lesson by offering external rewards, but when students are given freedom to design their own experiences, they have a tendency to take more ownership in their learning. This often presents a situation where motivation becomes intrinsic. For instance, when students are given the freedom to design projects of their choice, they usually develop projects that are relevant to their lives and therefore are motivated to complete them. Bruner (1960, p. 50) sums it up as follows: "If it is our intention as teachers to inure the child to longer and longer episodes of learning, it may well be that intrinsic rewards in the form of quickened awareness and understanding will have to be emphasized far more in the detailed design of curricula." Desire is internal and propels the student forward in the learning process. It is the catalyst that ignites learning and carries the student to the end of the project. Students are less likely to see the relevancy when subjects are compartmentalized and when subject matter is not necessarily of their interest but of the teacher's or school's interest.

When interest is internal, as opposed to being forced, students become both emotionally and intellectually invested in the learning process. Dewey notes, "Interest is in the closest relation to the emotional life, on one side; and through its close relation . . . to the intellectual life, on the other side" (1973, p. 422). Educators must tap into a student's emotional side in order to initiate the learning process. It appears that the primary aim of formal education is often focused on attaining content, which tends to sever emotions from the learning process, resulting in a lack of desire and motivation. When students choose experiences that are meaningful to them, they become excited and pursue learning on their own. In essence they become self-directed learners.

Interest is critical at the outset of the learning process, but educators may need to guide the process so that interest continues throughout the duration of the experience. When students are able to visualize their end view or goal, they can direct their efforts toward achieving this end.

The means used to reach this end may require students to undergo a series of trial-and-error episodes before they accomplish a task or complete a project. It is during the trial-and-error phase that educators may need to provide information and resources that allow students to overcome barriers they face. Otherwise students may lose interest, and important learning opportunities may be lost.

Educators can foster the learning process by asking students driving questions and providing appropriate problems that will help them maintain interest. Not enough challenge may result in boredom, and too much challenge may result in frustration. In either situation, learning may come to a halt if the educator does not provide appropriate guidance.

This does not mean that educators should provide the answers when students get stuck; rather they should provide resources that will allow students to move forward in their search for solutions. Instead of providing answers to be memorized for a test, this process allows students to make mistakes and learn to solve problems by making these mistakes. Experiential learning is sometimes arduous and may require extra time because students often make numerous mistakes along the way, but the learning may ultimately have greater meaning. Educators should place equal emphasis on the means and the ends. Projects and experiences, as opposed to worksheets and other academic exercises, tap into students' interests and allow them to work through a problem-solving process in order to complete their goals.

PRIMARY AND SECONDARY EXPERIENCES

Dewey (1973) was one of the earlier thinkers to discuss the difference between primary and secondary experiences in the educational process. He suggests it is necessary to "draw attention to the relationship between the objects of primary and of secondary or reflective experience" so that secondary experiences, such as those found in a textbook, do not become abstract and disconnected from primary experiences (p. 254). Primary experiences are direct experiences, which often require hands-on involvement. Common school examples include field experiences, internships, extracurricular activities, skills, and sports. Students are actively involved in the learning process, often experiencing things for the first time. Dewey argues that such experiences are extremely important: "An ounce of experience is better than a ton of theory simply because it is only in experience that any theory has vital and verifiable significance. An experience, a very humble experience, is capable of generating and carrying any amount of theory (or intellectual content)" (1916, p. 144).

Secondary experience, on the other hand, often results from primary experience. When individuals engage in a craft, such as carpentry or pottery, they reflect on past experiences to improve future projects. Or, when people participate in a sport, they reflect on how to improve future performance. Books and articles are often filled with examples of primary experiences that, when reflected upon, become secondary experiences. Right now you are reading this book, which will hopefully lead to reflection (secondary experience) that may help you implement more meaningful primary experiences for your future students.

As a former professor of undergraduate education, I had opportunities to experiment with different teaching approaches using a combination of primary and secondary experiences. In a Philosophy of Outdoor Education course I taught, I began the semester with secondary experiences (book readings and discussions), followed by primary experiences that required students to teach an outdoor activity to the rest of the class. Readings focused on topics such as experiential learning, physical and emotional risk taking, moral education, and facilitation techniques. During the first eight classes students read and discussed these topics, and for the last eight classes students were in the field teaching these skills to each other.

One problem with this approach was the difficulty of holding discussions during the first eight classes because many of the students had no previous primary experience with outdoor education activities. Most had never been exposed to outdoor activities such as rock climbing, canoeing, backpacking, or camping, so they were not able to discuss common philosophical underpinnings. This became evident when I asked them why they were having a difficult time discussing the material; most responded by stating they could not make sense of the philosophical information because they had no prior experience participating in outdoor activities.

I used a variety of discussion techniques mentioned in Brookfield and Preskill's book *Discussion as a Way of Teaching* (1999) without much success. This book is filled with ideas on how to generate discussion; however, undergraduate students often lack primary experience, which renders these techniques ineffective in such situations. The book readings in my Philosophy of Outdoor Education course were not understood at the time they were assigned because students lacked primary experience with this topic. The most common theme in my semester end evaluations focused on the idea that direct experience was much more meaningful than the book readings.

This personal experience prompted me to switch the sequence and provide students with a series of primary experiences at the outset of the course, followed by secondary experiences. In the next semester, students participated in a variety of outdoor activities during the first eight classes, and the last eight classes were dedicated to book readings and discussions. This approach proved to be much more effective; when students began reading and discussing the books during the latter part of the semester, they were lively and excited. Many even took issue and debated some of the theories found in the books.

Brookfield and Preskill's discussion techniques were much more effective with this group of students because they could relate to the theory. It was obvious from my semester evaluations and class discussions that students not only enjoyed the primary experience portion of the course but, by having it at the outset, also were better able to understand theoretical information (secondary sources) when it was presented.

Hutchings and Wutzdorff (1988) encountered this same phenomenon when examining an introductory course on social systems offered by the sociology department at Alverno College. When theory was presented first, "students repeated theories but did not apply them to their own experiences and lives. The instructors got the best results by leaving theory until later and beginning with students' experience, and instead of building theories out of air, building theory on that experience" (p. 11).

These examples imply that classroom educators may want to introduce students to primary experiences before book readings. For instance, history teachers could reenact a battle before reading about the Civil War, English teachers could ask students to perform shortened versions of plays before reading the classics, and physical education teachers could have students experience physical activities before reading theories of motor development and the benefits of exercise. Dewey explains it this way: "The subject matter of primary experience sets the problems and furnishes the data of the first reflection which constructs the secondary objects. . . . It is also obvious that test and verification of the latter is secured only by return to things of crude or macroscopic experience" (1973, p. 254). In other words, when students begin the learning process with a primary experience, it allows them to connect theoretical ideas to the primary experience, which in turn can be used to improve their own future primary experiences.

Educators that have been exposed to numerous and varied primary experiences often search for more secondary experiences that will help them improve upon their practices. Individuals with a wealth of primary experience, such as classroom teachers, may prefer to be offered secondary experience at the outset of an academic course instead of more primary experience. In one of my graduate courses, which usually consists of seasoned educators, the main assignment requires individuals to teach a lesson using an experiential format. Students must engage the rest of the class in experiential learning, which may be a bit daunting if they have never used this process. The primary experience (i.e., teaching the lesson) occurs at the end of the course. Readings and discussions (secondary experience) at the outset of the course provide these students with opportunities to gather information, ideas, and theories on how to implement their experiential learning lesson. This approach allows individuals to gather new ideas and theories, which they then apply to a future primary experience.

Unlike traditional education, which typically supplies students with only secondary experiences, students engaged in experiential learning incorporate both primary and secondary experiences into the learning process. Depending on the past experiences of the students, primary experience may be needed at the outset of the course, followed by secondary experience or vice versa. The main thing to remember as an educator, however, is to combine primary and secondary experiences within the same academic course. Learning may be lost if students are not given the chance to reflect on primary experiences and, likewise, when students are not given opportunities to apply information from secondary experiences.

INTERDISCIPLINARY CURRICULUM

Whitehead (1929) may have been one of the earliest philosophers to re-ject the separation of subject matter into individual classes and to sup-port the use of an interdisciplinary curriculum: "Our modern system, with its insistence on a preliminary general education, and with its easy toleration of the analysis of knowledge into distinct subjects, is an equally unrhythmic collection of distracting scraps. I am pleading that we shall endeavor to weave in the learner's mind a harmony of patterns, by co-coordinating the various elements of instruction into subordinate cycles each of intrinsic worth for the immediate apprehension of the pupil" (p. 21). Whitehead was urging educators to help students tie ideas together so that knowledge could become practical and useful. To do this, however, educators needed to cross over into other subject matters.

Today educators are still arguing in support of curriculum integration. In her book *Becoming a Better Teacher: Eight Innovations That Work*, Martin-Kniep (2000) mentions four reasons why curriculum should be integrated: "1) growing support for learning and assessment experiences that require the application of knowledge rather than memorization and accumulation of facts; 2) increasing understanding of how the brain processes information through patterns and connections with an em-phasis on coherence; 3) emerging awareness that knowledge is neither fixed nor universal, and that problems of real significance cannot be solved out of a single discipline of knowledge; and 4) the belief that an integrated curriculum can help teachers and students overcome rigid and arbitrary perceptions of subject boundaries" (p. 8). Curriculum must be integrated when using experiential learning because problems often arise requiring individuals to seek out information from multiple disciplines.

For instance, I was involved in a spaghetti bridge-building contest for high school students across the state of Michigan. Students needed to gather and apply physics, math, and carpentry knowledge in order for them to build the strongest bridge possible out of two pounds of spaghetti. They drew upon physics to determine the strongest structural designs, math for measuring trusses and roadbed sizes, and carpentry to build wooden jigs for specific pieces of the bridge. Teams often relied on input and feedback from math, physics, technology education, and a host of other teachers. One spaghetti bridge held more thean 40 pounds before breaking!

When individuals are engaged in such experiences they are applying their knowledge, making connections between different subject matters, solving relevant problems, and breaking down barriers between disciplines just as Martin-Kniep suggests. They are not memorizing facts, nor are they prohibited from using whatever subject matters are necessary to solve the problem; they are gathering information, trying out their ideas, and reflecting on whether the solution is adequate.

When subject matters are compartmentalized, learning may become disjointed and quickly lose meaning: math for 50 minutes, then history, then science, then English, and so on until the end of the school day, when students are left wondering how it all connects and what it all means on a personal level. High-stakes tests place teachers in a situation where they must provide students with very specific content. This situation does not provide incentive or the necessary time to help students connect one content area to the next. Lesson plans often have specific objectives such as learn a formula, remember dates of battles, or write a haiku poem. Such objectives are much easier to assess than whether a student has learned to think critically and solve real-life problems.

Life does not consist of segmented subject matter. It requires individuals to use an interdisciplinary approach when solving problems. Marzano states that "what we know about learning indicates that instruction focusing on large, interdisciplinary curricular themes is the most effective way to promote learning" (1992, p. ix). For instance, a curricular theme such as "telling stories," where students interview elders at a nursing home for the purpose of writing a book, would include learning about history, English, journalism, and potentially a host of other subjects. Students would learn living history as they hear stories of the past. They would learn how to conduct interviews and record information—in essence, how to become a journalist. They would learn how to write well in order to write stories about the lives of the people they interviewed. They could potentially learn many other things, such as geographical information about where people traveled and information about various occupations.

Unfortunately, many educators would tend to take each of these subjects and create narrow objectives, such as learn how to write a term paper, learn how to conduct an interview, learn the history of a specific country—and none of these objectives would be connected through an actual experience. When individual objectives are not connected to a relevant practical experience, they may lose their meaning and become forgotten.

Life is filled with complex problems that require individuals to solve them using a variety of subject areas. Experiential learning utilizes an interdisciplinary approach to education because when students directly experience something, they are exposed to a variety of subjects that are linked together. This process does not compartmentalize knowledge; instead it allows students opportunities to connect subject matters, ultimately seeing a bigger picture of how things are interconnected in the world.

KNOWLEDGE THAT RESULTS FROM EXPERIENTIAL LEARNING

Gardner (1993) identifies different types of intelligences, such as linguistic and bodily–kinesthetic, which implies that individuals may be more adept with one style of learning over others. For instance, one may be more adept at learning via linguistics and less with kinesthetics. Although an individual may be more adept with linguistic learning than bodily–kinesthetic learning, he or she may need to use both in order to solve certain problems.

The nature of reality requires us to solve problems, and solving problems requires a combination of thinking and doing. In many cases, we need to use our bodies as well. Understanding that there are multiple intelligences may help individuals identify specific learning preferences, but according to Hutchings and Wutzdorff (1988), experiential learning "involves and engages a range of domains—the cognitive faculties, of course, but also the kinesthetic, affective, ethical, attitudinal, and behavioral dimensions of learning. Learning acquired through several modalities is more likely to 'stick' as psychological research has clearly confirmed" (p. 12).

Whether you are training a dog, raising a child, fixing a car, or writing a book, they all entail using a variety of learning domains to solve problems.

We think and then test our ideas to discover solutions. Experiential learning combines theory with experience and mirrors reality because it requires individuals to solve problems by applying information. The process begins in the present and moves the students into the future toward the unknown.

Activities, projects, and field-based experiences require students to solve problems and search for solutions, which allows them to be discoverers of knowledge. A project is developed based on an interest, a search begins that includes solving problems that arise, and a process of thinking and doing occurs simultaneously that allows students to discover answers unknown to them. This process requires students to think for themselves and solve real-life problems. Most occupations require problem-solving skills; however, traditional education often emphasizes the skill of memorization. When educators start in the present but then move backward to the past by asking students to remember information that others have already discovered, knowledge is static. Students in traditional education settings are often provided with the answers rather than questions and problems.

Caine and Caine (2001) describe the traditional education process as follows: "Raising standards tends to mean adding more and more to the prescribed curriculum; improving teaching tends to mean ensuring that more and more educators follow a prescribed methodology; and holding teachers and schools accountable tends to mean allocating rewards or punishments according to how well students do on standardized tests" (p. 4). Knowledge in this context implies that the more you can remember the smarter you are. Problem solving is not required in this theory of knowledge; however, once students leave school and enter the job market, they are expected to think for themselves and solve problems. In school they memorize theory, but in society they are expected to apply it. These are very different theories of knowledge.

The process of planning, observing, testing, and reflecting is much more encompassing than sitting passively remembering information. Experiential learning requires students to get up out of their chairs and test out their ideas in real-life situations. For instance, how can one learn to be an effective educator without actually teaching?

The definition of knowledge must include direct experience because "a theory apart from an experience cannot be definitely grasped even as theory" (Dewey, 1916, p. 144). Activities, projects, and field-based experiences require students to explore the unknown. The starting point is a question or problem that leads the students into the world searching for answers and solutions. Knowledge in this context is dynamic. Much knowledge changes over time, which is why the learning process should start at the present and move forward into the future, allowing students opportunities to solve problems so they may become self-directed learners before entering the job world.

Some educators assume that younger students learn differently than adults and are not intellectually capable of engaging in a more involved theory of knowledge. Wald and Castleberry (2000) identify the following five assumptions that they suggest are unique to adult learning: "inquiry into underlying assumptions deepens the learning process, learning is an active process that occurs over time, learning is driven by the learner around meaningful issues, learning is experimental by nature, and learning is fueled by rich, diverse, accessible sources of information" (p. 9). These assumptions imply that younger students learn differently, yet one could argue that these five assumptions are common to all learners. Problems will vary tremendously in difficulty, but the process is the same.

For instance, my wife, who formerly taught fifth grade, told me a story about her school's science teacher, who helped students build a device to pull balls and objects off the school roof. He started the project by asking students to identify one of the most significant problems they faced at their school. Most agreed that it was frustrating to wait for custodians to get the ladder out to retrieve objects off the roof. Students, along with the guidance of their teacher, designed and built a retrieval device to solve their problem. The problem was relatively simplistic in nature, but the process required a lot of planning, thinking, and doing before they were satisfied with the end product. One could easily argue that the assumptions of active learning, pursuing a meaningful issue, experimenting, and relying on accessible sources of information apply just as readily to these fifth graders as they do to adult learners when attempting to solve problems. Similarly, in higher education it appears that professors often assume undergraduate students learn differently than graduate students. Undergraduates are not viewed as self-directed learners, so classes are usually more structured. For instance, lecture courses usually meet several times a week, are teacher directed, and require daily readings and assignments to keep the students on track.

Graduate courses, on the other hand, usually meet less often for longer periods of time, often use a seminar format, and include self-directed activities and projects. Graduate students are often given the freedom to pursue their own learning and are more readily allowed to engage in experiential learning opportunities. If educators want students to be thinkers rather than memorizers, they must embrace a theory of knowledge that is dynamic and allow students freedom to plan and apply their ideas to solve problems relevant to their individual lives.

MOVING TOWARD THE FUTURE

Much of the literature on experiential learning comes from fields within higher education. Undergraduate and graduate programs in outdoor education use this learning process because students learn outdoor skills, such as rock climbing and orienteering, by directly participating in them. Adult education uses this process because adults prefer to be active learners (Wald & Castleberry, 2000), and service learning uses it because students learn about themselves and others through direct experiences with citizens in their communities (Cousins & Mednick, 1999). Why is there not more literature on how to use experiential learning with high school and college students? Barriers seem to be mounting: less time, more structure, less money, more tests. There is little reason or incentive for educators to change from a passive learning to an active learning format when accountability depends heavily on high test scores.

Some schools and educators are challenging traditional education by leaving the system and creating new schools that allow for more experiential learning. For instance, Dennis Littky, who helped create the Metropolitan Regional Career and Technical Center (the Met), designed an experiential school with internships, projects, and exhibitions. It has been highly successful, with its first senior class of 46 receiving "a total of 90 acceptance letters from Brown, Reed, Northeastern, Worcester Polytech, University of Rhode Island, Community College of Rhode Island, and 20 other colleges from Vermont to Arizona" (Levine, 2002, p. 132).

Ron Newell and Dee and Doug Thomas were key creators of the Minnesota New Country School (MNCS), which uses an experiential approach called project-based learning (Newell, 2003). This is an individual approach to education that allows students freedom to follow their interests. The system they have created looks nothing like the systems in traditional schools. The school has large open spaces for larger group work and computer workstations for each student. Not only is the educational philosophy unique, so is the way in which the school is governed. Advisors wear many hats and may take on the role of school official one day and custodian the next, which promotes an attitude of ownership among the staff. MNCS has been extremely successful and received a Bill & Melinda Gates Foundation grant in 2000, resulting in the creation of several more project-based schools.

Greg Farrell (1999) helped create Expeditionary Learning Outward Bound (ELOB) schools. He borrowed some of the guiding principles from the wilderness-based Outward Bound schools such as service, adventure, compassion, and character to develop schools where teachers and students create and implement learning expeditions. These expeditions engage students in a sense of adventure as they design and implement service projects that require groups of students to work together as cohesive teams. Students not only learn content knowledge but also discover new things about themselves, others, and the world they live in. ELOB schools have expanded to include elementary, middle, and high schools and have spread in numbers across the country as well.

Finally, at Souhegan High School, under the guidance of founding principal Robert Mackin, students are at the center of the learning process (Silva & Mackin, 2002). All decisions made at this school fall back on a key component of the mission statement, which is "maximize learning for all students" (p. 51). This school has incorporated project-based learning and allows students to follow their interests to develop and exhibit their projects. Students have a strong voice in many of the decisions made at this school, which has led to the creation of numerous experiential learning opportunities.

It is unfortunate that school reformers leave traditional education settings in order to create meaningful change because the masses are in traditional settings. But, maybe as schools such as the Met, MNCS, ELOB, and Souhegan continue to prove their effectiveness, traditional schools will take notice and begin implementing some of the ideas developed by these highly experiential schools. As Dewey (1938) notes, change in the schools continues to be a slow process, but with continued persistence reformers such as those mentioned in this chapter might be able to convince traditional educators to use more experiential learning in their classrooms.

4

EXPERIENTIAL SCHOOLS

Metropolitan Regional Career and Technical Center (the Met), Minnesota New Country School (MNCS), Expeditionary Learning Outward Bound (ELOB), and Souhegan High School are four school reform movements that have fully integrated experiential learning into their school curriculums. All four use a combination of activities, projects, and field-based experiences coupled with the pattern of inquiry to create learning environments that mirror the way individuals learn when they are no longer in school. Some schools focus more on projects, whereas others place primary emphasis on field-based experiences, but they all focus on placing students in situations where they must test their ideas against reality and solve real-life problems.

I chose to describe these four school reform movements because students at these schools are engaged in experiential learning almost all the time. It is not something that only certain teachers use or that is included only in specific courses; it is at the heart of their educational philosophies. Students learn by doing. They solve real problems that crop up while pursuing activities, projects, and field experiences. Although there are times when teachers may lecture in order to provide students with needed information, direct experience still drives the learning process.

The information presented in this chapter describes some of the philosophical underpinnings of these schools, as well as key aspects behind how these schools function. Specific ideas and examples from these schools are included because they have the potential to be implemented in traditional classroom settings. Educators in more traditional settings wishing to implement experiential learning may want to start slowly, choose one or two ideas most practical for their school environments, and build on these ideas as time goes by.

METROPOLITAN REGIONAL CAREER AND TECHNICAL CENTER (THE MET)

The Met uses a combination of activities, projects, and field-based experiences to promote experiential learning; however, learning through internships (LTI) appears to be at the heart of this school's philosophy (Levine, 2002). The school is extremely unique in that its entire curriculum is based on experiential learning. There are no class periods or bells. Students may attend several meetings during any given day depending upon their learning progress. Students at the Met belong to an advisory, which consists of 14 students and one advisor. Advisors stay with these students through their four years of high school education. They meet with their students once in the morning and once in the afternoon, when students are not out doing internships to listen to short presentations on a variety of topics, as well as to discuss student learning plans. Advisors also meet with students frequently in one-on-one situations to discuss ongoing progress. The advisor's primary role is to help guide students through their various activities, projects, and internships during their high school experience.

Each student also has a learning team, which includes the advisor, internship mentors, and parents. The learning team meets quarterly to help students develop learning plans outlining their activities, projects, and internships. The following questions are used to help students when developing their learning plans:

- What are your interests?
- What experiences and skills would you like to gain?

- What are your strengths?
- What areas do you need to work on?
- What are your goals after high school?
- How do you learn best? (Levine, 2002, p. 97)

Designated time is set aside for students to present their projects and internship experiences to their learning team when completed. A mix of subjective and more objective assessment tools are used to determine whether a student should be allowed to move on to the next project or internship.

One of the key tenets to the Met's educational philosophy is to discover interests, which helps motivate students to complete their learning plans. The Met uses a variety of activities to help students discover their interests. Here are some examples:

- Create a past life journey map of your important life experiences, people, hobbies, special talents, group activities, music, books, movies, beliefs about society, jobs, good times, hard times, things from your culture (art, language, tradition, rituals, religion), and anything else that has shaped the way you think and act.
- Create a future life journey map. What do you want your life to look like 2, 5, 10, and 25 years from now? Include employment, education, hobbies, skills, travel, spirituality, character, and location. Imagine your retirement party. You have accomplished your most important life goals. Who is there and what are they saying about you as a person? What are they saying about the events of your life?
- What are the greatest sources of suffering in the world? In your country? In your community? What are the most critical needs that are going unmet? Which businesses, organizations, or individuals are involved in solving these problems?
- See or play a movie that interests you and explore it in depth: read the history of the period. Why were the clothes like that? Compare the language from then with now. Read a biography of the main character. Dig deeper into anything that grabs your interest.
- Talk with more experienced students about their passions. How did they figure out what they liked to do? Do the same thing with parents, relatives, neighbors, church members, and retired adults.

Other activities include scavenger hunts, skill inventories, career interest checklists, library and Internet searches, oral histories of people of interest to students, autobiographical sketches, and family histories (Levine, 2002, p. 31).

At the Met, these activities help students discover their interests and are also used as a vehicle to help them identify potential internships. Educators in more traditional school settings may wish to use some of these ideas to tap into students' interests, which may then be used to help students develop and implement projects and activities.

Learning through internships (LTI) provides students with field-based experiences that allow them to explore different career possibilities. Students work closely with mentors who help them identify specific skills they wish to learn. Internships are not used specifically for learning a vocation, but instead are used as a way for students to learn important life skills. Students are expected to participate in one internship per year and may choose dramatically different internships from one year to the next. Internships ground students to reality and help them realize the importance of developing life skills that are necessary to do well in any occupation.

Projects are one of the key tools students use at the Met to demonstrate what they are learning. Projects consist of varying complexity; for instance, some may take a week to complete, whereas others may take a year. Independent projects tend to be shorter in length and are often used to help students find internships; senior projects, which are required of all seniors, take a full year to complete. In addition, projects are part of the internship process. Each internship requires a project consisting of three components: "an end product for the internship host site, an investigation related to that product, and the student's critical reflection on the learning process" (Levine, 2002, p. 47).

In addition to activities, projects, and internships the Met provides students with opportunities for service learning, journal writing, public speaking, enrolling in college courses, and test-tasking preparation. Students receive a list of annual expectations, as well as a specific list of expectations for their own grade levels. Completing these expectations requires students to rely heavily on the experiential learning process.

Annual Expectations to Be Completed Every Year

- Follow interests in the real world (informational interviews, job shadows, and LTIs).
- Obtain LTI during the first semester.
- Have a positive impact on the community (service learning, etc.).
- Meet the learning plan team at least three times per year.
- Be aware of gaps in learning and address them through project work.
- Create at least four learning plans per year.
- Complete the work in learning plans.
- Build a binder of best work and a portfolio of all work.
- Have four public exhibitions per year.
- Write in journals three times per week.
- Schedule daily planners every week.
- Come to school on time every day.
- Be responsible for actions and locations; sign out of advisory.
- Show respect to self and others.
- Take responsibility for the learning process.
- Take advantage of opportunities.
- Make productive summer plans. (Levine, 2002, p. 98)

MINNESOTA NEW COUNTRY SCHOOL (MNCS)

Another excellent example of a school that has embraced the philosophy of experiential learning is the MNCS. This charter school uses a project-based approach to education, which allows students to create and implement projects that are meaningful and relevant to their lives. The school allows students opportunities to determine what they want to learn and how they want to learn it, to be creative problem solvers, and in the end, to apply what they are learning. Project-based education utilizes the principles of experiential learning because it "emphasizes student interest rather than following a fixed curriculum; emphasizes a broad, interdisciplinary focus rather than a narrow, discipline-based focus; uses direct, primary, or original sources rather than texts, lectures, and secondary sources; [and] emphasizes data and materials developed by students rather than teachers" (Newell, 2003, p. 5).

Similar to the Met, students at MNCS are assigned to an advisory group with one advisor who helps them create and develop their projects. Parents and guardians play a pivotal role at MNCS by signing off on project proposals and exhibitions. In addition to advisor and parent/guardian support, students have an assigned project planning group, consisting of peers and other interested individuals, that guides them through the process from beginning to end. The advisor's primary role is to help students create and complete their projects. The number of credits attached to each project depends upon the complexity of the project. The project-based process requires students to submit a project proposal, document their progress, and present completed projects in the form of an exhibition to their advisory group. The following project proposal outline was taken from Ron Newell's book *Passion for Learning* (2003, p. 101).

Project Proposal Form

1. Project Title: _____
2. Topic to be researched or investigated: _____
3. List at least three basic information/fact questions you would like to answer concerning your project:

   _____

   _____

4. How does this project apply to life outside of school? What makes this project important to the community/world around you? (At least two reasons):

   _____

   _____

5. Brainstorming (may choose between A and B or do both):
   a. Develop a web (attach)
   b. Design an outline (attach)
6. Tasks/activities to complete this project and dates to complete by:

   _____

   _____

   _____

7. List a minimum of three types of resources you will use. At least one of these must be a primary source (living person):

_____

_____

_____

8. List the standards (high school graduation requirements) that will be validated after project completion (need to have applicable standards copied, highlighted and attached to proposal form):

_____

_____

_____

9. Number of project credits (must have documented hours/work to receive credit): _____

10. Initial proposal approval:
    Parent/Guardian: _____ Date: _____
    Advisor: _____ Date: _____
    Project Planning Group: _____ Date: _____

11. Checklist needed to be completed before final approval:
    - Documentation of project learning
    - Time log
    - Project checklist (if needed)
    - Works cited/bibliography
    - Performance rubric
    - Summary/reflection (Describe the process of completing what went well and what you would do differently. How did the project affect you as a student, a citizen, and/or family member?)

12. Final Approval:
    I agree my child's project is ready for final approval
    Parent/Guardian: _____ Date: _____
    Advisor: _____ Date: _____
    Project Planning Group: _____ Date: _____

Number of Documented Hours: _____

Actual Project Credits: _____

Letter Grade: _____

The project proposal form does an excellent job walking students through the entire project process from beginning to end. The proposal form engages students in the pattern of inquiry from the very outset of the project. It immediately taps into students' interests by allowing them freedom to choose a topic of their choice. It then asks students to identify three questions they would like to answer and how the project is relevant to them and the world. Students develop problems they would like answered and in the same breath begin brainstorming potential solutions to these problems. The proposal includes terms such as activities, tasks, and primary resources (i.e., people), which allows students to think about how they might incorporate activities and field-based experiences into their learning in order to complete their projects. The project drives the curriculum, and information is obtained only when needed to complete the project.

The proposal also gets students thinking about how their learning will be assessed. For instance, it asks students to identify the Minnesota graduation standards that will apply to the project, along with the rubric forms that need to be filled out to determine if students have met these graduation standards. In addition, students are asked to keep a learning log documenting their time spent working on their projects, which is also used as part of the assessment process. Finally their projects must be approved by their project committees, and before signing off on the completed projects, students must present them to their project committees. Ultimately each project committee determines whether the student has completed the project worthy of his or her capabilities.

EXPEDITIONARY LEARNING OUTWARD BOUND (ELOB) SCHOOLS

The philosophy behind expeditionary learning is based on some of the same principles created by Kurt Hahn when he developed the first Outward Bound school in Great Britain (Farrell, 1999). Outward Bound is a wilderness school that combines adventure with service as a way to promote personal growth. Expeditionary learning schools use adventure and service as metaphors to foster an environment where students learn to solve problems by working together in small groups, while at the same time building character by pushing each other beyond their pre-conceived boundaries to achieve higher levels of learning.

According to Campbell, expeditionary learning is about creating "long term, in-depth investigations of a topic that engage students in the world through authentic projects, fieldwork, and service" (1998, p. 3). A learning expedition may include projects, fieldwork, and/or service, but more important is the learning process in which students work together to solve problems and push one another to greater levels of understanding.

There are four key components to a learning expedition: learning goals, guiding questions, projects, and assessment. Learning goals focus on learning specific content, skills, and qualities of character and community. For instance, if fly fishing was an expedition topic, learning goals might include identifying what insect hatches occur during different times of the year (content), learning how to cast a fly rod (skill), and teaching young children to tie flies (community). These goals provide students with opportunities to learn more than just content, which is typical of many traditional school classroom settings.

Guiding questions are developed by the educators initially but may be altered by students as they begin to flesh out their learning expedition. These questions are used as a vehicle to help students focus their interests and develop problems that will challenge their minds and bodies. Questions are often the starting point in the expedition but may change as goals and projects are developed. For instance, an initial question might be "How does one create a web page?" but as a student begins to work on this project, he or she may raise another question, such as, "How does one design a user-friendly web page?" Questions that may hold more meaning arise as the learning process unfolds.

Like the Met and MNCS, ELOB schools use projects as their centerpiece to learning. Educators and students design projects based on real problems, then present their projects to an outside audience when completed. Projects include a service component, which makes them relevant, practical, and meaningful to all involved in the process because they directly impact everyone involved.

Expedition teams consisting of students and teachers work together to plan out learning expeditions and service projects. Although teachers ultimately determine service projects, they "ensure that students have the experience of making meaningful choices within the service project" (Campbell, 1999, p. 3). State and district standards to some degree drive the design of the learning expedition; however, student ideas are relied upon to create the design as well. ELOB schools encourage parents and other community members to get involved in expeditions. Service projects often result from community involvement. Assessment is an ongoing process where educators and students provide ongoing feedback to one another during the process. Portfolios and exhibitions at the conclusion of projects are the two primary tools used to assess student work. A typical learning expedition plan outline follows (Campbell, 1998, pp. 33–43):

Topic

Guiding Questions

Learning Goals (refer to state and district standards when creating Learning Goals)

Students will understand . . . (knowledge of content)

Students will practice and be able to do . . . (skills and habits)

Students will practice and develop qualities of character and community, including . . .

Projects:

A learning expedition may include one major or a few smaller projects

Project Description(s)

Learning Goals Addressed by Project

Major Activities/Steps (steps leading to the completion of the project)

Specific Goals for Activities/Steps

Ongoing Assessment (specific strategies you intend to use within this project)

Assessment:

Final Assessment: Performance or Presentation of Learning

(Describe assessment of individual or group projects such as debates, galleries, exhibits of work, oral presentations of portfolios of project work, play performances, or final essays or research papers)

Assessing Students' Overall Achievement (by what standards will you and the students assess learning and define quality work and achievement on the learning expedition as a whole?)

Resources:

> Develop a list of resources that will anchor the content of the expedition, including books, speakers, "experts," fieldwork sites, project materials, and so on.
>
> Books, Articles, Literature (select titles for required and optional reading)
>
> Experts (who are the experts who could help plan, visit the classroom, or be contacted by individual students?)
>
> Fieldwork Sites (what sites can be visited by the whole class and/or small groups of students?)
>
> Project Materials and Equipment

Like the other schools, the ELOB learning process poses questions at the outset, which creates an atmosphere of research and discovery. Students must identify questions that require searching for answers. This immediately places the students in a state of perplexity to discover the unknown. In addition, all three schools reverse the teaching format, using a problem-solving process of learning as opposed to a lecture format.

Once the appropriate questions are identified, students are asked to identify learning goals, which requires them to look forward and determine specific outcomes they would like to accomplish. Projects and assessment techniques are then created, leading students into a journey of planning, testing, and reflecting. Similar to the other schools, teachers provide guidance along the way, helping students continue forward toward accomplishing projects and, ultimately, their learning goals.

SOUHEGAN HIGH SCHOOL

While teaching at the University of New Hampshire in the spring of 1993 I received a phone call from Alan Gordon, the guidance counselor at Souhegan High School, asking if I would be interested in facilitating team-building activities for the faculty at this school. He was primarily interested in providing new faculty (they were all new in the fall of 1992 when the high school first opened its doors) with an opportunity to get to know one another. He is still a strong advocate of using team-building activities, especially with advisory groups at the school, to help build stronger bonds. "We needed to involve ourselves in team building activities that would quickly form us into closely knit faculty" (Silva and Mackin, 2002, p. 56). As a young faculty member new to the area, I was eager to begin networking with area schools, so I was delighted to have this opportunity. Over the next couple of months, Alan and I talked about my participation in the teacher orientation program at this school. He mentioned that the school was new as of the fall of 1992, and they were involved in a school reform movement based on some of the Coalition for Essential Schools principles developed by Ted Sizer (1984, 1992). I knew some of the principles behind this school reform movement were aligned with Dewey's philosophy of education, and even though my role was very minor, I was still excited to facilitate activities to enhance group cohesiveness, as well as have an opportunity to discuss the theory of experiential learning.

Today the school has gained national recognition and has been replicated by several other schools. The guiding principles of this school are as follows:

- A clearly articulated mission to drive the actions of the school
- Heterogeneous grouping and inclusion of all students
- Core curriculum with "less is more" philosophy
- Curriculum based on essential questions
- Teachers acting as coaches/facilitators
- Advisory groups at all grade levels
- Emphasis on interdisciplinary curriculum
- Honors challenges available to all interested students in all classes
- Teams of English, math, science, and social studies teachers at grades 9 and 10
- Interdisciplinary teams of teachers, if possible, at other grade levels, including a mandatory senior seminar
- All teams having common blocks of teaching time and of planning time
- All classes meeting for at least one extended time block during the week
- An integrated math program in grades 9–11
- An integrated science program in grades 9–10 at least
- An adventure-based physical education program

- An integrated arts program
- Technology integrated into core curriculum, not separate classes
- Foreign language built on a communicative approach
- Performance assessment (with clearly defined rubrics) and portfolios expected of all students
- Senior project as a culminating exhibition for all graduating students
- Professional development built on teacher collaborative work
- Democratic decision making, including a Community Council with student voice
- Grading based on A, B, C, system, anything less than a C– not to receive credit (NC)
- No departmental structure (Silva & Mackin, 2002, pp. 27–28)

As in the other previously mentioned schools, questions and problems drive the curriculum. Instead of passively taking notes, each student assumes the role of researcher and discoverer. This process occurs not only in individual classrooms but in the larger school community as well. "Whole-school conversations about issues of concern to students and adults offer a catalyst for reflection, debate, and action" (Silva & Mackin, 2002, p. 49). Students not only have a certain amount of freedom to follow their interests within the classroom but can also be actively involved in the larger decisions that affect and impact the entire school.

After the general school principles were developed, classroom practices were designed to guide the learning process in the classroom. The following is a list of the classroom practices:

- We focus on essential questions rather than textbooks.
- We focus on authentic contexts for our curriculum.
- We focus on performance-based assessments.
- We focus on including all students in our curriculum.
- We offer Honor designations to students in every classroom.
- We focus on collaboration with our peers.
- We focus on reflection in our daily practices.
- We focus on involving colleagues in our work. (Silva & Mackin, 2002, p. 53)

These classroom practices drive home the point that memorizing facts from textbooks is a less important skill than critical thinking. Students and teachers work together to solve problems and questions in the classroom because learning is seen as a mutual undertaking. Building relationships between students and teachers is vitally important and is the reason learning has become fun and exciting for everyone at this school.

With approximately 1,000 students, Souhegan is much larger than the Met, MNCS, and many of the ELOB schools, but larger student numbers have not deterred them from implementing several key concepts that lend themselves to experiential learning opportunities. One is the advisory group consisting of one advisor and 10 to 12 students. Advisory groups meet every day for 25 minutes to discuss issues concerning academic progress and personal growth. Even though the primary focus is to foster communication skills, team building, trust, and individual self-esteem, advisors also help students with their division-one exhibition and senior projects. These small group settings provide students with one-on-one attention that allows advisors to help students move forward with their projects, portfolios, and exhibitions.

Division-one exhibitions occur at the end of the sophomore year. Students create a portfolio of their work from the 9th and 10th grades, which they present to their "roundtable"— consisting of peers, teachers, parents, and community members—in a 45-minute time frame. Advisors help students compile the portfolios, choosing different papers, essays, and other schoolwork that represents their learning progress in these two grades. Advisors ask questions about strengths, weaknesses, and commitment to learning, which helps students analyze past experiences and how these experiences may be applied to future learnings. Students also write letters reflecting on their learning and how it applies to the school's mission statement, as well as to potential directions for new learning. These letters allow the roundtable to understand how students are connecting past experiences to present and future learning interests. At the conclusion of the exhibition, members from the roundtable are allowed to ask questions, for the purpose of helping students identify personal and academic areas of growth in the present and for the future.

The senior project is an extensive research project that entails identifying a question or problem of the student's interest, reading and researching the topic, interviewing experts on the topic, and giving a 20-minute presentation focusing on research methods. Here are the minimum expectations for the senior project:

- Sixty hours of documented research time.
- Written notes resulting from personal interaction with human resources, such as a formal interview, internship, apprenticeship, and shadowing of or with an expert on the topic of the project.
- Use of printed resources, including books, technical literature, and appropriate articles from reputable sources.
- Deadlines and appointments with mentors, advisors, and others associated with the project will be met.
- Notes from printed resources will include more than just highlighted or underlined passages and must contain a personal synthesis of relevant information.
- An annotated bibliography must include a minimum of 10 citations form a variety of sources.
- At least two thoughtful and dated entries in the learning narrative each week from the beginning of the project to the end.
- All narrative entries will be word processed.
- Project binder will be organized according to guidelines and will properly reflect active research. (Silva & Mackin, 2002, p. 102)

Expectations for the senior project are somewhat like a thesis defense. Students write a proposal that their project team must approve, conduct their research with special attention given to methodology, present their findings to a panel, and write a reflection paper on what they learned from doing the project. They must identify a mentor from the school, as well as a community expert who agrees to help them with their project. Advisors, mentors, and experts communicate periodically to check on the students' progress. In the end, students have engaged in a number of activities and field experiences, allowing them to complete their projects. Numerous problems are solved along the way, which helps them become thinkers rather than memorizers.

All these schools are very much alike in that hands-on projects and internships drive the curriculum, and portfolios and exhibitions drive the assessment process. The focus for all four school reform movements is on providing students with primary experiences. Secondary experiences such as reading books and articles are used primarily for the purpose of applying them to primary experiences. For instance, a service project such as digging a garden for an assisted living facility will require students to read information about gardening techniques, seeds, growing seasons, tools, and so on. Such secondary experiences are needed in order to accomplish the primary experience.

Dewey notes that traditional education has the tendency to work backward to the past for the purpose of memorizing secondary experiences: "Books, especially textbooks, are the chief representatives of the lore and wisdom of the past, while teachers are the organs through which pupils are brought into effective connection with the material" (1938, p. 18). The learning process comes to a halt when experiences from the past are not projected into the future. For learning to occur, students must use secondary experience to create new knowledge, and creating new knowledge may mean moving beyond the four walls of the classroom, which the Met, MNCS, ELOB, and Souhegan have done. Interestingly, the National Association of Secondary School Principals' *Breaking Ranks* (1996) report mentioned in chapter one promotes some of the same ideas as these nontraditional schools.

> For years high schools have made minimal use of programs that reach beyond the four walls of the classroom: work-study, independent learning, distance learning, apprenticeships, mentorships, internships, job shadowing, independent study, field trips, travel, courses at college, student-conducted research. High schools should incorporate these approaches and others extensively into the education of students. The setting in which learning occurs—as measured by seat time—will matter less when high schools break free of the restrictions imposed on them by the Carnegie unit. Students should have the opportunity to demonstrate the value of credible learning experiences, wherever they occur. (p. 51)

Breaking Ranks II (2004) promotes the use of a "personal adult advocate" (p. 18), similar to the role of the advisor in small group advisories discussed earlier in the chapter, and a "personal progress plan" (p. 18), similar to the learning plans also mentioned previously. Traditional and nontraditional schools appear to be moving closer together in their educational philosophies, which will hopefully encourage educators in more traditional settings to explore and experiment with the ideas in this chapter.

5

USING EXPERIENTIAL LEARNING IN CLASSROOM SETTINGS

The four school reform movements discussed in chapter four had the freedom to create structures and systems that allowed their teachers and advisors to use experiential learning exclusively within their schools. Educators that work in more traditional settings do not have this luxury and are bound to a more rigid system that consists of short class periods where specific subject matters are taught. Educators in these settings have greater challenges to overcome when attempting to implement experiential learning and, therefore, might want to begin by implementing one or two ideas in this chapter in one of their classes and then branch out to include other classes, if possible. Using experiential learning is not always easy, but there are practical techniques and ideas that can be implemented in all classroom settings.

One way to begin thinking about using experiential learning is to first determine what teaching format you use in your own classroom. According to Coleman (1976, 1995), there is a distinct difference between the information assimilation teaching format used primarily in classroom settings and experiential learning. Information assimilation (IA), which is most commonly used in classroom settings, begins when educators present facts and information to students and is completed when students apply this information in reality (1976, pp. 50–51). Unfortunately, the application phase is often excluded from this learning process and replaced with a paper and pencil test. Lecture is the most common teaching format used with this learning process and is "traditionally relied heavily on" as the main teaching format (Fink, 2003, p. 3). Lecture, however, has been proven to be ineffective because students often lose focus and do not remember much of what was said during the class.

Research over the past 20 years supports this idea. For instance, in 1984 Pollio discovered that 40 percent of the time during a lecture, students are thinking about something other than what the professor is saying (p. 11). McKeachie (1999) suggests that lecture is less effective than discussion formats in "retaining information, transferring knowledge, problem solving, attitude change, and motivation for further learning" (p. 67), and Fink's (2003) more current analysis mirrors these findings by proposing that lecture is not only boring but also does not help students "retain information after the course is over, develop an ability to transfer knowledge to novel situations, develop skill in thinking or problem solving, or achieve affective outcomes, such as motivation for additional learning or a change in attitude" (p. 3). These studies imply that attention, retention, and ability to apply information continue to be sorely lacking in traditional classroom settings.

But of even more concern is what goes on in students' heads when they are attempting to retain information for exams. Students cram information into their brains, remember it for the test, and then quickly forget it afterward. Whitehead recognized this problem way back in 1929 when he stated, "Get your knowledge quickly, and then use it. If you can use it, you will retain it" (p. 36). When application and problem solving are left out of the learning process, students quickly forget information. Problem solving requires thinking and thinking requires work, and when you apply information to solve problems, you are more apt to retain it.

Even graduate students who have been away from academia for several years working as professionals in their fields have had the IA process so ingrained in them that they quickly revert back to old habits when returning to the classroom. An interesting phenomenon has occurred in some of my graduate seminar classes. Students began taking notes only after I got up from my chair and began writing ideas down on the board. Many assumed this information might show up on a test later in the course. I interrupted their note taking to make sure they understood that they would not be tested on the information, but instead should write down whatever information they might want to use in their own classrooms. After I made this comment, most students would relax and refocus on the information instead of taking notes.

The effects of IA on undergraduate students are even more evident. I have encountered many students that appeared to have forgotten how to think altogether. During attempts to hold philosophical discussions about teaching and learning, students would often respond to my questions by saying something like, "This requires too much thinking, can't you just give us the information and test us on it?" Book-smart individuals are a result of this process. Many educators probably know or have heard of straight "A" students who were able to remember facts for tests but unable to apply the information in reality.

Fink's (2003) taxonomy for significant learning, which includes "foundational knowledge, application, integration, human dimension, caring, and learning how to learn," promotes the use of a teaching format that incorporates problem solving and application (p. 30). He states that "aside from foundational knowledge, application is the second most important goal" in the taxonomy (p. 38). With information assimilation, students would be more apt to retain information if given opportunities to apply it. Unfortunately, it appears that educators spend much of their time doling out information without providing students opportunities for application. No wonder students lose interest in classroom settings when they are not challenged to think on their own and figure out how to apply information.

To help curb apathetic attitudes toward learning, educators should use a learning process that begins with problems and questions to be solved instead of a learning process that begins with information to be remembered. Caine and Caine (2001) agree. They argue that "the graduate model is simply a version of a good model that works best at every age. Guided experience relies, for example, on student research of topics that are personally interesting, and yet make it possible for the basics to be covered and mastered" (p. 114).

Think about the learning process you use most often in your own occupation. If you are an educator, you are constantly doing action research in an attempt to answer questions and solve problems on a daily basis. The "classroom press" describes in part teachers' experiences and how they are pressed to respond to and solve a variety of concerns and problems every day:

- The press for immediacy and concreteness: Teachers engage in an estimated 200,000 interchanges a year, most of them spontaneous and requiring action.
- The press for multidimensionality and simultaneity: Teachers must carry out a range of operations simultaneously, providing materials, interacting with one pupil and monitoring the others, assessing progress, attending to needs and behavior.
- The press for adapting to ever-changing conditions or unpredictability: Anything can happen. Schools are reactive partly because they must deal with unstable input—classes have different "personalities" from year to year; a well-planned lesson may fall flat; what works with one child is ineffective for another; what works one day may not work the next. (Huberman, 1983, pp. 482–483)

Educators are constantly answering questions and solving problems associated with activities, projects, and classroom experiences. As with most jobs, questions and problems are addressed on a day-to-day basis. Educators solve problems such as how to challenge all students, how to deliver content to mixed-ability groups, how to curb behavioral problems, how to accurately assess learning outcomes, and what to include in student portfolios. For teachers, much of their learning is driven by the questions and problems they face every day.

Educators typically do not have time to search out theory for the sake of learning theory. Theory does not drive the learning process, questions and problems do, and information is sought when it is needed. Theory that is presented at a time when it is not needed often lacks purpose.

For example, requiring math teachers to attend an in-service on how to implement a new curriculum a year in advance of when it is to be implemented would probably result in a waste of time. As it is, most of the money spent on staff development in the United States is "intellectually superficial, disconnected from deep issues of curriculum and learning, fragmented, and noncumulative" (Ball & Cohen, 1999, pp. 3–4).

Teachers are usually not interested in learning theory that has no connection or relevancy to their jobs and the specific problems that come with them.

Educators get upset when they are required to attend workshops and learn things that have little connection or relevancy to their jobs; yet this is often what they expect of their own students. They cover content that often lacks connection to students' lives. They also give students theories and information weeks, months, and sometimes even years before they have opportunities to apply it. Undergraduate education is probably most guilty of this situation. Many four-year programs provide students with multiple-theory courses. The information presented in these courses is typically supposed to be applied during a field experience, which usually occurs toward the end of the degree program. By the time students get to their field experiences, however, they have forgotten much of what they learned in the classroom and will have to relearn it during the field experience.

Educators continually gather information when they need it to solve problems, and life outside the classroom is no different. Life requires individuals to solve problems all the time. Therefore, it seems reasonable to suggest that educators should promote the use of a problem-solving process in their classes because this skill is essential to all human beings. The way to do this is to reverse the IA learning process. Instead of starting classroom lessons with information, educators should start with questions and problems.

Reversing the learning process is the first step to implementing experiential learning in the classroom. It has the potential to be much more effective than information assimilation and is a simple idea with significant ramifications for students and teachers. However, educators may need to reevaluate how they teach their classes and think creatively about how to reverse the learning process. Reversing teaching formats from information giver to problem poser changes what goes on in students' minds. Students begin thinking about how to solve problems, as opposed to blindly taking notes.

After teaching high school, undergraduate, and graduate students, I discovered one significant difference between undergraduate and high school students and graduate students. For the most part, undergraduate and high school students lack primary experience in their chosen fields.

Obviously, this is not true in all cases, but many students in this age range have not had opportunities to experience career interests firsthand, and so they are unable to make sense of theory because they cannot ground it in past experience. They come to school, are presented with ideas and theories that lack connection to their lives, and become disenfranchised with school because it lacks meaning in their personal lives.

Students in this situation need to be exposed to primary experiences in their academic courses. This is exactly what Expeditionary Learning Outward Bound, Minnesota New Country School, the Met, and Souhegan are doing: providing students with opportunities to explore their interests through primary experiences. Students at these schools understand they are aiming toward the completion of a project or a field experience such as an internship and therefore are involved in a learning process that requires them to gather information that will help them accomplish their aims. They have a vision of what they want to achieve from the outset and engage in a learning process that requires them to solve multiple problems along the way before reaching their end goal.

The following examples may provide readers with ideas on how to reverse the learning process by using the pattern of inquiry in classroom settings. Numerous examples of projects, activities, and field experiences may be found on the web (e.g., at www.wested.org/pblnet/exemplary_projects.html), so I will limit my suggestions to several examples from high school, undergraduate, and graduate education.

As mentioned in chapter two, projects require students to produce a document. Activities include presentations, discussions, simulations, debates, and role plays; field experiences occur outside the classroom, usually in conjunction with a professional in the field. For the examples provided here, I have chosen to focus more on projects and field experiences than activities for the following reasons: they are more in-depth, requiring greater amounts of work; they are the primary focus of these courses; and they are the culminating experience for students in these courses because they must present them to the class.

Because of a lack of time, field-based experiences may be more difficult to implement during actual class periods. However, in some cases, educators may be able to assign mini field experiences outside regular class time. I use a combination of activities, projects, and field experiences in my classroom courses, which provides variety and keeps students interested and involved in the learning process. In addition, certain subject matters, such as art and science, may lend themselves more readily to experiential learning; however, experiential learning can be applied to all subject matters with a little creativity. Educators should keep in mind that creating an experiential curriculum takes time. Finally, educators should remember that students do not need to leave the classroom to test out their ideas; they can be engaged in the pattern of inquiry in the classroom.

HIGH SCHOOL EDUCATION

I remember in 1989 being enthralled and fascinated while watching a TV program titled "The Truth about Teachers," which was aired on NBC and has since been turned into a video available at www.buyindies .com/listings/8/7/AIMS-8728.html. Some of the best teachers in the country were interviewed and spoke directly about *how* they taught their classes. Not one of them used the term experiential learning; yet they all were masters of the process. It appeared that in most cases their biggest concern was figuring out how to motivate their students to learn; and they did this through a process of trial and error. As some of them were being interviewed, they talked about how they kept trying different teaching approaches until they hit upon something that worked. Here are three examples from this program.

Joe Ryan, a history teacher, reenacted battles of the Civil War at Gettysburg. In his history classes, students had to make their own wooden guns, sew their own authentic soldier uniforms, and cook and eat food that soldiers ate during the war. Students had to study the battles in detail so they could reenact them in the way in which they actually happened. They also had to study the life of a soldier and learn such things as commands, marching instructions, and Civil War strategies. During the actual reenactment, which occurred toward the end of the course, everything was done as accurately as possible. Students loved the experience—and history came alive for them.

Ryan is still actively involved in providing field experiences for individuals, but today his students are teachers. He started the Living History Education Foundation, which trains teachers how to incorporate living history into their curriculums (www.nysut.org/newyorkteacher/2002-2003/030129history.html). The foundation is funded through a $300,000 state grant that helps offset the costs for teachers wishing to attend either week-long or weekend workshops that provide them with the same experiences they will expose their students to when they return to the classroom.

Science teacher John Barainca built a space lab in his classroom where students would spend up to a week at a time living the life of an astronaut confined to the lab. Students would perform small research studies, exercise, eat, and sleep in this small lab. Other students in the class acted as ground support and provided the astronauts with necessary information to complete their studies and accomplish their mission's goals. This simulation gave students a deeper understanding of space exploration, as well as some of the trials and tribulations of being an astronaut.

Like Ryan, Barainca is still at it today, only on a grander scale. He operates a mobile space lab unit and offers simulated flight experiences to Mars. He has been offering these types of experiences to high school and college students for 29 years. He has taught astronomy at the Salt Lake Community College and is also a member of the Mars Mission Support team, which has a website offering a variety of educational opportunities for teachers (www.marssociety.org/MDRS/team/msupport.asp).

Perhaps the most famous example from "The Truth about Teachers" program is *Foxfire* magazine, created by Elliot Wigginton and his high school English classes in 1966. He asked his students at Rabon County High School in Georgia to go out into the rural areas around the town and interview their grandmas, grandpas, aunts, uncles, and other relatives and neighbors to collect information about local folklore. Students wrote stories about the folklore and lost arts of this mountain region through the voices of the elderly and put them together in a magazine, which they published and distributed around the community. The magazine became so popular that students under Wigginton's guidance began putting these stories together and publishing them in a book format. Today there are a total of 11 books, with another due out in October 2004.

Starnes (1999) discusses the enormous ramifications this teaching approach has had on education in the United States:

> While its original emphasis was on teaching high school English through oral history, today's Foxfire Approach is used in all grade levels and all content areas. It enlivens the learning process by giving students and teachers rich experiences. The process bridges the theoretical perspective of Dewey's writings and the practical work of teaching. Through their interrelated nature, each adds to the understanding and power of the other, making genuine experience the driving and connecting force of classroom learning. (p. 6)

Teachers all over the country are using writing projects similar to *Foxfire* to engage students in direct experiences outside the classroom. Students in these programs must find people in their communities that have interesting historical backgrounds and convince them to tell their stories. The writing project (i.e., books or magazines) drives the learning process and requires students to experience firsthand how to interview and write accurate stories about these people.

These three individuals make excellent examples of how teachers can reverse the learning process, allowing students to become problem solvers and active learners. Reenacting a Civil War battle, spending a week inside a space station, or writing a magazine provides students with long-range, concrete goals that require them to solve multiple problems. They understand what they are aiming toward and can assess their progress along the way. When projects, activities, and field experiences are clear and concrete, such as the ones just outlined, students know what they need to do and, with guidance from their teacher, can overcome challenges and problems they face.

In addition, these examples are true testimonials to the effectiveness of experiential learning. At minimum, Ryan has been using this teaching approach for 15 years, Barainca for 29 years, and the *Foxfire* approach has been around for 38 years. Good educators use things that work. If something doesn't work, they discard it and try something different until they hit upon an approach that is effective. These educators continue to use this approach because students of all ages appreciate learning through direct experience with the subject matter.

UNDERGRADUATE EDUCATION

College educators have more academic freedom than high school educators to incorporate projects and experiences into their curriculums; however, many college courses may be limited to shorter time frames, much like high school classes. Here are some examples from my own undergraduate courses that can fit within these shorter class periods.

One comes from a course I taught in risk management. Most of the students in this course came from the fields of outdoor education and recreation services; however, several local business people took the course as well once they discovered how it was being taught. This course used an extensive project combined with several mini field experiences as the driving forces behind the learning process. The project consisted of developing a risk management plan for an actual organization of the student's choosing. However, to develop this plan, each student had to visit the site of the organization and spend time with the director, discussing the facility and the various programs provided by the organization. In some cases multiple meetings with the director were necessary in order to fully understand the facility and its programs.

Classroom discussions in this course focused on issues such as legal liability, negligence, and conducting various activities, which were then implemented into their risk management plans. We used a book on legal liability and risk management as a tool to develop solid risk management plans. Midway through the course, students had to turn in a rough draft of their risk management plans to me, as well as to the organizations, to make sure they were on the right track. This occurred at the end of the course as well. In addition, they had to turn in a log documenting their time at the facilities working with the directors.

These mini field experiences working with these organizations opened the students' eyes to the professional world and made many of them realize the magnitude of responsibility associated with being a director of one of these organizations. They also realized that their projects were not just academic exercises to be turned into their professor but were living documents that would be implemented by these directors. Evaluation for these projects rested ultimately with the directors. If they approved, full credit was awarded; if not, further work would be needed.

It became obvious to the students that accurate information was vitally important to their projects, but their field experiences and projects—not the book readings—were driving the learning process. A dramatic shift in thinking occurred when students realized that the purpose of their projects was to provide safe policy and procedures for these organizations, so the information contained in these documents had better be accurate. Information becomes important when it has practical application and becomes relevant to the lives of those it affects.

Experiential Activities for the Classroom is an example of an undergraduate course where I used several field experiences at the end of the semester to guide the learning process throughout the course. The primary objective of this course was to teach students how to facilitate team-building activities in classroom environments. Team-building activities used in this course require participants to practice skills, such as problem solving, communication, compromise, and risk taking. The facilitator's role is to explain objectives, rules, and safety procedures of the activities and then facilitate a discussion with the participants to enhance learning outcomes.

I mentioned to students at the outset of the course that their field experience would consist of facilitating these activities with math students at the local high school during the last several class periods of the semester. Every class session up to that point focused on preparing students to facilitate these activities. Two types of experiences were provided to prepare them for their field experiences. First, I facilitated a number of team-building activities so that students could learn the activities and understand why skills, such as communication and cooperation, are important in problem solving. Second, students practiced facilitating these activities with each other so they could practice verbalizing rules and safety precautions, as well as practice leading discussions after the activities were completed. Participating in the activities and practicing their facilitation techniques provided them with the skills needed to facilitate these activities with high school students.

Projects and field experiences, such as the preceding two examples, contain in them a variety of problems to be solved. For instance, when developing a risk management plan for a fitness center, students had to figure out how fitness instructors should be hired and trained, what the safety protocols are for using a weight room, and what procedures should be in place if someone goes into cardiac arrest. When educators assign major projects and field experiences at the outset of an academic course, problem solving, rather than memorization, is elicited. This is a reversal from the information assimilation process. A relevant problem is presented first rather than information to be memorized. Projects and field experiences with their many subproblems require students to engage in the pattern of inquiry, combining thinking with application. This is a critical first step when implementing experiential learning. When educators understand this notion, they can begin developing an experiential curriculum to fit their specific subject matter.

GRADUATE EDUCATION

Graduate students often return to school with a fair amount of primary experience and are searching for ideas on how to improve their practices. They are not necessarily looking for more primary experience, but instead are searching for secondary experiences they can apply back in their own classes. In this situation, discussion is often an effective teaching format. I use a combination of individual and group presentations and small and large group discussions. The focus, however, of all these presentations and discussions is on application. In other words, my role as an educator is to engage students in the pattern of inquiry, leading them to a point where they actually test out their ideas against reality, thus learning experientially. Secondary experience may be used more heavily with graduate students, but the focus is still on how to become a better practitioner.

For instance, a classroom teacher of 10 years does not need to be exposed to more classroom experiences before reading about different learning theories. He or she needs to be provided with ideas, resources, and techniques to take back to the classroom for experimentation. I use book discussions at the outset of graduate courses, not only to challenge students' thinking but also to help them formulate ideas for their projects and presentations at the end of the course. Reversing the learning process by posing questions and problems is still central to the course, even though more secondary experiences are used with graduate students.

I am fortunate to work in a graduate degree program that consists of a combination of classroom, project-based, and field-based courses. The project-based and field-based courses are independently designed by the student in consultation with his or her advisor and are usually completed off campus. For instance, Experience and Education and Development of Experiential Education are strictly project-based courses; internship and practicum courses are field based. For these courses, students are required to fill out learning contracts, complete their projects or experiences, and write reflection papers that address their learning outcomes. There is no seat time in a classroom with these courses. Even though separate courses are designated as project based and field based, I still incorporate projects and mini field experiences in my classroom courses as well.

One example of how I reverse the learning process with graduate education comes from a course called Experiential Education and School Reform. The main focus of this course is a significant project where students design a curriculum with assessment tools, which they present to the class at the end of the course.

The focus of this course from the very beginning to the very end is on completing their projects, and to do so students must solve multiple problems along the way. A variety of presentations that students may apply toward their projects are used throughout the course. One type, called individual mini presentations, consists of two- to three-minute presentations on their interpretation of the required book readings. Book topics include learning theories, designing authentic curriculums and assessment tools, project-based education, and designing field-based experiences. During these individual mini presentations, no one else can talk except the presenter. Once everyone has completed their presentations, an open discussion with the whole class occurs. These mini presentations provide all students with an uninterrupted opportunity to express their ideas on the readings. Large group discussions focus on how the book readings can be applied to their curriculum projects. Used in conjunction with book readings, the mini presentations and group discussions generate ideas that others may wish to implement.

Another activity I use in this course is what I call "working sessions." For these class sessions we meet in a research lab at the library, and students work on their curriculum projects using the Internet and other library resources. Students work for about an hour and then report out to the large group. The focus of these report out sessions is to identify specific problems people are experiencing so the class can brainstorm and provide potential solutions to these problems. This activity is very useful in helping students continue moving forward with their projects. At the end of the course, students present their curriculums and assessment plans. The rest of the class has an opportunity to ask questions and provide written feedback that may help students further refine and improve their projects.

Activities such as presentations, discussions, and working sessions are fueled with questions and problems that students must solve in order to move ahead with their projects. Students are researchers and discoverers of their own knowledge. I do not provide the answers; students search and discover their own solutions.

Another example comes from a course called Organization and Systems Change. This course focuses on a variety of topics such as organizational development, systems thinking, organizational models, and the change process. During the first class period, students discuss the change process by answering questions such as the following: What is change? Why do organizations and individuals avoid change? What are advantages and disadvantages of change? During the second class, students focus on identifying a project that will change their organizations for the better. Together students help one another by brainstorming, discussing, and refining their projects. Once students refine their projects they begin working on them, and they present them to the class at the end of the semester. From this point forward, the focus of the course is on completing their projects.

Students choose from a wide range of project topics such as developing or refining policy and procedures, creating staff manuals, developing web pages, developing marketing materials, and developing new curriculum activities, to mention a few. At the end of the semester, students are usually excited and motivated to share their projects because they are relevant to their jobs and, in many cases, help make their work more manageable and enjoyable.

Students demonstrate their knowledge and understanding of the change process via their presentations, which usually range from 20 to

30 minutes in length. Questions and discussion follow the presentations, allowing students to further refine and improve upon the changes they are in the process of making within their organizations.

The project becomes the driving force behind the learning process in this course, and information is utilized only when it is needed to move the project forward. There are no exams, so information does not need to be memorized, but students do need to know how to obtain necessary information so they can apply it toward their projects if necessary.

These are only a few examples of projects, activities, and field experiences that high school and college teachers can implement in their courses. As mentioned before, hundreds of activities, projects, and field experiences may be found by searching the Internet. One of the key concepts, however, to effective experiential learning is to assign a challenging project or field experience at the outset of a course that students must present at the end of the course. This places students in a situation where they must collect information, develop plans, and solve problems as they work toward completing them. This process falls in line with Henry's (1989) definition of project work: "an extended piece of work in which the student (or group of students) is required to select a topic, collect relevant information, and organize this material into a presentation" (p. 32). Books and other materials are used as resources to solve problems, as opposed to being used as a source of information that must be memorized for tests. Readings and discussions occur throughout the semester so that students can gather and apply information toward their projects. As the process unfolds, students will find that they are motivated, interested, and excited to share their findings with the rest of the class.

SUGGESTIONS TO ENHANCE EXPERIENTIAL LEARNING IN CLASSROOM SETTINGS

In summary, I would like to make a few simple suggestions that may help educators guide students through their projects and field experiences.

1. Assign one major project or field experience to guide learning throughout the course. When you have one major assignment, it provides students with a clear goal to accomplish and keeps them

moving toward achieving this goal. It also keeps the project or field experience at the forefront of the learning process and becomes the driving force behind everything the student does in the class. Educators often require students to do projects and turn them in at the end of the course but fail to spend any class time working on them or discussing progress. From my experience, it seems to be more effective when time is dedicated to the project or field experience every class period. In my risk management course, for example, each class period was dedicated to a specific piece of the risk management plan. We would discuss the topic of the day to make sure everyone understood the concepts, and the remaining time was dedicated to working on risk plans in small groups. This format provided students with opportunities to raise questions and discuss various pieces of their risk plans, which ultimately allowed them to produce more accurate documents. When students know what they are aiming toward, they understand that each class has purpose because it provides a stepping-stone toward that overall aim. They understand the bigger picture and are more easily able to see how each class moves them closer to their goals.

2. Combine projects, activities, and field experiences when possible. When you combine all three in a course, it provides variety and keeps the class interesting and engaging. One major assignment, such as a project, usually necessitates the need for students to engage in activities and field experiences. For instance, the risk management plan mentioned earlier required students to go into the field and interview directors of various organizations. To produce accurate documents, students needed to venture out into their communities and interview directors. The project necessitated a field experience. This adds value to the overall process and creates a more holistic learning process.

3. Choose activities, projects, and field experiences that are challenging yet manageable. I like to give students some choice in determining what they want to do, but I also provide them with a generic framework so they understand what is expected of them. In my school reform course, I suggest that their projects entail developing a curriculum with outcomes and assessment tools. Students have the freedom to choose content area, length and depth

of curriculum, outcomes, assessment techniques, and so on. Even though I choose the overall idea behind the project, they have the freedom to determine everything else about the project. Likewise, in my philosophy course, I choose the culminating experience, which is to teach a lesson to the class using an experiential approach to education, but students choose the topic, activities, and teaching approach. From my experience, students will often create challenging activities, projects, and experiences when given some freedom to choose things they are interested in. The educator's role is to help keep projects and field experiences manageable so that students carry them through to the end.

4. Provide clear expectations. With graduate students I give fewer expectations because I want them to figure out what is most meaningful to them. I don't want them to give me what I want, I want them to give me what they want. Graduate school is often a stepping-stone to a higher level position, which often means taking more advanced leadership roles that require greater problem-solving skills. I want students to leave graduate school confident in their abilities to take risks and solve problems on the spot. Too much guidance may hinder this process. On the other hand, undergraduate and high school students may need more and clearer expectations. When I was teaching undergraduates, I often provided a list of activities, projects, and experiences from previous courses. This was a valuable and popular resource because many had no idea what they wanted to do. In addition, I would give them more specific expectations. For instance, in the risk management course I provided an outline of things to include in the risk plan such as philosophy, activities and safety protocols, emergency procedures, evacuation plans, and contact information. I also required students to meet with the directors of these organizations so they could have ongoing conversations about the details of the risk plan.

5. Tie the curriculum to projects and field experiences. Class readings and activities should be directly tied to the project or field experience. Educators should consider the readings and activities as resources that will help students accomplish their projects or experience. In my organization and systems course, the open space

dialogue activity allowed students to brainstorm and eventually identify their change project. From that point on in the course, everything we did in class was related to their projects. Readings focused on the change process and how to implement change in different settings. One primary question that was raised frequently after class discussions was, "How can you implement this information into your change project?" Time was often set aside in class to discuss this question in small groups so that students could begin formulating ideas for their project design. Likewise, in my school reform course I used readings on experiential learning theory, curriculum design, outcomes, and assessment tools. Every reading was useful in helping students design their experiential curriculums. For instance, after discussing a reading on developing learning outcomes, students would work independently for a period of time, developing outcomes for their curriculums. Students would come back together at the end of the class period and do a quick report out on their progress. This time was also used to discuss problems students were facing, along with potential solutions.

6. Changing directions midstream is allowed. Students often start out with one project idea but, as they proceed, discover they are more interested in a different topic. I want them to do a project that is meaningful and practical. If they are frustrated or lacking in interest, I encourage them to change directions and pursue something they are passionate about. I have had students start developing one curriculum and change to another halfway through the semester. The amount of time they have to complete the project is obviously a consideration, but if the project is not meaningful, it becomes another academic exercise that might not ever be put to practice.

6

ASSESSING EXPERIENTIAL LEARNING

Standards-based and performance-based assessments are two common approaches used to measure student learning. Standards-based assessments focus on mastery of content, which is determined by using standardized tests. Performance-based evaluations also focus on mastering content, but learning is based on the student's ability to apply information, so rubrics are commonly used to determine the level of understanding. This chapter discusses these two approaches to assessment and provides examples of assessment tools, plans, and reports that may be used with experiential learning.

Over the past several decades, billions of dollars have been spent on the production and use of standardized tests (Stiggins, 2002). They have long been the primary assessment tool to measure mastery of academic content because they provide hard data that can be used to rank and categorize students, schools, and school districts. More recently, standardized test scores have been used to hold teachers accountable for their teaching effectiveness. According to Reeves (2004), "the prevailing assumption is that test scores, typically reported as the averages of classes, schools, or systems, are the only way to hold teachers accountable. Teachers know, of course, that their jobs are far more complex than what can be measured by students' performance on a single test, and they understandably resent the simplistic notion that their broad curriculum, creative energy, and attention to the needs of individual students can be summed up with a single number" (p. 5).

Roeber (2002) agrees that test scores should not be tied to teacher effectiveness, nor should they be used as the only assessment tool to measure student achievement. He suggests classroom educators, specifically those tied to content areas, should de-emphasize test taking and instead emphasize "application and use of content, even to the point of advocating not teaching certain content" (p. 172). Newman, Secada, and Wehlage (1995) voiced even stronger opposition by suggesting that standardized tests should not be used because they are "considered trivial, contrived, and meaningless by both students and adults" (p. 7). A growing number of assessment experts suggest that the field of education move away from using standardized tests, if not eliminate them altogether, and instead search for tools that measure performance and application of information (Serow, 1998; Newman, Secada, & Wehlage, 1995; Roeber, 2002; Reeves, 2004).

Which side of the debate between standards-based and performance-based assessment one agrees with depends on how one defines knowledge. If one views knowledge as the ability to memorize information, then standardized tests will be considered more accurate than other assessment tools. On the other hand, if one views knowledge as the ability to apply information, then performance-based assessment tools such as rubrics and self-assessments will be the tools of choice.

There are arguments for and against both types of assessments. Proponents of the No Child Left Behind act may argue that standardized tests are more objective because there are definite right and wrong answers. Exact scores can be determined, which eliminates subjectivity on the part of evaluators. For instance, it may be difficult for evaluators to determine whether students should be scored at a level three or four on a performance-based tool such as a rubric. Proponents of the *Breaking Ranks II* report, on the other hand, may argue that performance-based assessments require higher order thinking skills such as problem solving, which is an important life skill. Applying information is viewed as being more useful than memorizing it. Performance-based assessments may be more encapsulating because one needs to memorize, or at least remember information, in order to apply it, and therefore standards-based assessment skills are included. For instance, it is difficult to apply a theory, formula, or technique if you can't remember it.

Experiential educators support performance-based assessments because they view knowledge as the ability to apply information, which often requires using life skills such as communication, cooperation, risk taking, and problem solving. For instance, when teaching students about Shakespeare, an experiential educator might ask students to act out one of Shakespeare's plays, which would also require them to communicate, cooperate, take risks, and solve problems. When mastery of academic content is viewed as the ability to memorize information, then it would not be necessary for students to act out the play. Students could write down different lines of the play on a test and receive a high grade, but if they act out the play they will gain a deeper understanding of the story, as well as receive an opportunity to practice important life skills.

Another problem with standards-based assessment, according to Airasian and Abrams (2002), is the assumption that one test can measure mastery of content for all students across a particular grade level. Most U.S. states have created minimum standards that students are tested on to determine where they rank in comparison with other students, schools, and school districts. This presents a problem for experiential educators who promote a learning process based on application and learning from direct experience.

Going back to the Shakespeare example, a student could learn a great deal about Shakespeare's plays and play acting via direct experience yet fail a standardized multiple choice test about Shakespeare. A particular student may not do well on a test that asks for specific dates, names, and places yet do extremely well when asked how the play applies to his or her life, or what was learned about him or herself while acting out the play. Unfortunately, certain students may have a good understanding of the main plots and themes that run through Shakespeare's stories but lack specific pieces of information necessary to receive a high score on a standardized test. Standardized tests might allow for objective scores across a grade level, but evaluating student achievement may require using a self-assessment tool that asks individual students what they learned from a specific lesson or experience.

When students apply information, they go through a process of constructing knowledge from their own experiences. Experiential learning is aligned with the constructivist theory of learning in that "the outcomes of the learning process are varied and often unpredictable" and "learners play a critical role in assessing their own learning" (Lambert et al., 1995, p. 18). What one student takes away from an experience may be different from what the next student takes away. For instance, one student might gain confidence from conquering stage fright while acting in a play, whereas another might gain a deeper appreciation for the classics. This implies that without the appropriate assessment tool, such as a self-assessment, the educator might not ever realize that significant learning occurred. Therefore, classroom educators should search for assessment techniques that measure more than just the ability to remember information.

According to Serow (1998), assessment techniques based on one's ability to apply information are more appropriate and effective for experiential learning. For instance, self-assessment tools such as reflection papers, learning contracts, and student interviews allow students to identify important learning outcomes and place students in a participatory role evaluating their own learning. It seems reasonable to include students in the assessment process, for who better knows what they have learned than the students themselves?

Stiggins (2002) agrees and offers an alternative to the standards-based approach by identifying three ways to get students involved in assessing their own learning:

- Student-involved classroom assessment
- Student-involved record keeping
- Student-involved communication (p. 35)

Student-involved classroom assessment allows students to define how their work will be judged. Depending on age level, students wouldn't necessarily determine specific learning outcomes, but they could help determine what criteria would be used to judge their work. They might create a rubric and therefore would know exactly what they need to do to reach various levels of performance on the rubric. Student-involved record keeping allows students to keep track of their work. An example would be a portfolio, which shows how students have progressed over time. Student-involved communication allows students to present their learnings to an audience such as with exhibitions or student-led conferences. Level of understanding can be more easily assessed when students are required to express their ideas and present their learnings in a public forum.

Student-involved assessment fits well with experiential learning because it allows students to determine what criteria are most important to them. For instance, students might decide that learning specific life skills such as risk taking and communication are as important as learning academic content, and this could be built into the assessment tools. In addition, self-assessment techniques mirror the philosophy of experiential learning because students are actively involved in the process. They can be involved in creating criteria and performance levels for assessment tools such as rubrics, as well as collect examples of their work, which can then be presented to an audience.

Roeber (2002) has identified three assessment techniques I use in my experiential education graduate courses: performance tasks, constructed response exercises, and portfolios that incorporate student-involved assessment (p. 172). Performance tasks require students to demonstrate their knowledge through presentations, exhibitions, and projects. Constructed response exercises may be self-assessments that entail writing reflection papers on specific learning outcomes. For instance, learning contracts that I use for some of my courses ask students to identify learning outcomes they wish to achieve, and when they have completed their experiences, write reflection papers addressing their learning outcomes. Portfolios are a collection of student work that might include essays, reflection papers, projects, and written evaluations, often used to show how students have improved over a given period of time.

EXAMPLES OF PERFORMANCE TASKS, CONSTRUCTED RESPONSE EXERCISES, AND PORTFOLIOS

The experiential education graduate program at Minnesota State University, Mankato (MSU, Mankato), consists of a combination of classroom, project-based, and field-based courses. Classroom courses are seat-based seminars that meet once a week for three hours during the semester. These courses incorporate a variety of activities including discussion, individual and group presentations, projects, and lectures. Project-based courses are designed by the student in conjunction with an advisor and are done independently off campus; field-based courses consist of experiences such as practicums and internships completed off campus, typically under the guidance of a supervisor. In addition to completing course requirements, students must complete a thesis, alternate plan paper, or capstone project. Assessment tools have been created to evaluate learning outcomes for these different courses.

Rubrics have been developed to assess performance tasks for some classroom-based courses in the Experiential Education program. They were designed using Newman, Secada, and Wehlage's (1995, p. 8) notion of authentic achievement, which consists of "constructing knowledge, disiplined inquiry, and value beyond school."

For instance, in my Experiential Education and School Reform course, knowledge is constructed as students work on real-world problems that require problem solving through trial and error and ultimately have value in the world outside of school. Students design an experiential curriculum that includes identifying topic areas and planning out how they would teach classroom lessons experientially, presenting their curriculums by explaining learning outcomes and assessment tools and discussing how classmates can use this information in their own learning environments outside the university. The construction of knowledge, disciplined inquiry and value outside the classroom are assessed as students present their curriculums to the class.

The rubrics used in the Experiential Education and School Reform course to assess learning outcomes can be found in figures 6.1, 6.2, and 6.3. The rubric in figure 6.1 is designed to assess the student's level of understanding through written and oral expression. The rubric in figure 6.2 is similar to figure 6.1 but is used to assess the quality of written and oral presentations, and the rubric in figure 6.3 is designed to assess demonstrations and written expressions of student projects. These three rubrics are used to assess not only Experiential Education and School Reform projects but other experiential education classroom courses as well.

Student's Name _____

Professor or Advisor's Name _____

Construction of Knowledge: Demonstration of Understanding				
Rubric Descriptors	**Novice**	**Acceptable**	**Admirable**	**Exemplary**
	Shows a little understanding of ideas or processes. The concepts, evidence, explanations, arguments, questions posed, and methods used are inadequate for the issues and problems examined. Responses reveal major misunderstandings of key ideas or methods. 1	Shows a novice to limited understanding of ideas or processes. The concepts, evidence, explanations, arguments, questions posed, and methods used are somewhat simple or inadequate for the issues and problems examined. Responses may reveal some misunderstandings of key ideas or methods. 2	Shows a solid understanding of ideas or processes. The concepts, evidence, explanations, arguments, questions posed, and methods used are appropriate for the issues and problems examined. Responses reveal no misunderstandings of key ideas or methods. 3	Shows a sophisticated understanding of relevant ideas or processes. The concepts, evidence, explanations, arguments, questions posed, and methods used are advanced for issues and problems examined. 4
Demonstration of Understanding through Written Expression				
Demonstration of Understanding through Oral Expression				

Figure 6.1. Rubric for master's in experiential education: Construction of knowledge—demonstration of knowledge through written and oral expression. Adapted from G. Wiggens (1998).

Educators can hand out rubrics at the beginning of the course so students know what they will be assessed on and what they need to do in order to achieve the higher levels of mastery. Educators should keep in mind that most assessment tools have their disadvantages, and rubrics are no different. Dennis Littky, one of the principals at the Met (discussed in chapters three and four) cautions against using rubrics by

Student's Name _____

Professor or Advisor's Name _____

Construction of Knowledge: Demonstration of Quality				
Rubric Descriptors	**Novice**	**Acceptable**	**Admirable**	**Exemplary**
	The performance or project is ineffective. The performance is unpolished, providing little evidence of planning, practice, or consideration of audience. The presentation is unclear and confusing so that key points are difficult to determine. **1**	The performance or project is somewhat effective. Some problems with clarity, thoroughness, and delivery are evident. It is unclear whether the audience, context, and purpose have been considered. **2**	The performance or project is effective. Ideas are presented in a clear and thorough manner showing awareness of the audience, context, and purpose. **3**	The performance or project is highly effective. Ideas are presented in an engaging, polished, clear, and thorough manner. A high-quality craftsmanship is evident and is mindful of the audience, context, and purpose. **4**
Demonstration of Quality through Written Expression				
Demonstration of Quality through Oral Expression				

Figure 6.2. Rubric for master's in experiential education: Construction of knowledge—demonstration of quality through written and oral expression. Adapted from G. Wiggens (1998).

stating, "In the end, even with rubrics, someone has to make a series of subjective decisions, such as whether an essay is organized at an average or advanced level" (Levine, 2002, p. 116). This suggests that the question of how well educators are measuring what they think they are measuring in classroom settings still remains unresolved.

Constructed response assessment tools have been created for project-based courses, as well as experience-based courses such as practicums and internships. These constructed response exercises are learning contracts that address specific learning outcomes identified by the student

Student's Name_____

Professor or Advisor's Name _____

Disciplined Inquiry for Project-Based Learning				
Rubric Descriptors	Novice	Acceptable	Admirable	Exemplary
	The performance or project is ineffective. The performance is unpolished, providing little evidence of planning, practice, or consideration of audience. The presentation is unclear and confusing so that key points are difficult to determine. 1	The performance or project is somewhat effective. Some problems with clarity, thoroughness, and delivery are evident. It is unclear whether the audience, context, and purpose have been considered. 2	The performance or project is effective. Ideas are presented in a clear and thorough manner showing awareness of the audience, context, and purpose. 3	The performance or project is highly effective. Ideas are presented in an engaging, polished, clear, and thorough manner. A high quality craftsmanship is evident and is mindful of the audience, context, and purpose. 4
Disciplined Inquiry for Project-Based Learning: Project Demonstration				
Disciplined Inquiry for Project-Based Learning: Reflective Written Expression				

Figure 6.3. Rubric for master's in experiential education: Disciplined inquiry for project-based learning—project demonstration and reflective written expression. Adapted from G. Wiggens (1998).

doing the project. They guide students through the inquiry-process pattern by asking them to explain their projects and identify several learning outcomes they hope to achieve, as shown in the following Project Proposal Form. Answering questions on this learning contract allows students to think their way through the pattern of inquiry before beginning, which helps eliminate wasted time on ideas that are not practical. The leading contracts include reflection papers that provide valuable insights into how students view their own learning progress.

**Project Proposal Form for
ExEd 603 Experience and Education and
604 Development of Experiential Education**

Name:
Course number:
Semester that I am registered for this credit:

LEARNING CONTRACT
1. What is the problem or question I will address?
2. What resources will I need to help find an answer?
3. What is my plan to solve this problem or question?
4. How will I put this project into action? How will I implement this project?
5. What are the learning outcomes I wish to achieve?

ASSESSMENT
After completing the project write a reflection paper assessing what you learned and whether you achieved your learning outcomes. Note: Another assessment tool may be used in addition to the reflection paper.

To receive a grade for this project students must send a completed learning contract either as an attachment or a hard copy, and when finished with the project a brief reflection paper addressing your learning outcomes.

I use learning contracts in my field-based courses as well. For instance, in my practicum and internship courses students begin the process by discussing with me what they want to do for the course. Once the practicum or internship has been agreed upon, students fill out a simple learning contract answering who, what, where, when, and how questions. In this contract students must identify specific learning outcomes they wish to accomplish. After finishing their field experience, they submit a reflection paper addressing whether or not they achieved their outcomes listed on the learning contract.

Field-Based Experiences Learning Contract for ExEd 634 Practicum, 635 Internship, and 677 Individual Study

Name:

Course title:

Semester that I am registered for this experience:

LEARNING CONTRACT

- Who will I be working with and/or for during this experience?
- What will I be doing during this experience? What are my job responsibilities?
- Where will this experience occur? How much time will actually be in the field? How much time will be in an indoor environment?
- When will this experience occur? What is the beginning and end date?
- How will I accomplish this experience?

    List the learning outcomes you hope to achieve during this experience: _____

ASSESSMENT

When you have completed the experience write a brief reflection paper on what you learned and whether you achieved your learning outcomes. Note: Another assessment tool may be used in addition to the reflection paper.

To receive a grade for this experience students must send a completed learning contract either as an attachment or a hard copy, and when finished with the experience a brief reflection paper addressing your learning outcomes.

Graduate students enrolled in field-based courses often want an assessment of their work performance from their immediate supervisors. You will notice in the field-based learning contract that students have the option to use other assessment tools in addition to the reflection paper. For this reason, students enrolled in field-based courses are provided with a

Unaware	Novice	Intermediate	Professional
Behaviors do not reflect the disposition. May be unaware of need for disposition.	Behaviors begin to reflect the disposition. However, implementation is not always consistent or successful.	Behaviors consistently reflect the disposition.	Behaviors frequently go above and beyond expectations. Shows leadership or passion. Engages in proactive behavior successfully.

Dispositions	Behaviors	Assessment Level			
		Unaware	Novice	Intermediate	Professional

Domain A: Planning and Preparation

View each person as unique	Shows awareness and appreciation of others' varied approaches to learning/diverse interests				
	Shows awareness and appreciation of others' abilities, strengths, culture, linguistic heritage				
	Shows awareness and appreciation of others' stages of development				
	Selects appropriate and inclusive assessments				
Comments:					

Domain B: Learning Environment/Work Climate

Open to views of others	Interacts positively				
	Views things from others' perspective				
Expect the best	Establishes clear and appropriate expectations of self and others				
Comments:					

Figure 6.4. Assessment form for Minnesota State University's experiential education program. Source: C. Danielson, 2002.

Domain C: Teaching/Leading for Learning

Engaging	Designs learning activities that actively engage students/participants/clients				
Connecting school to life	Implements appropriate instructional strategies, activities, and assessments for real-life situations				
Flexibility	Monitors and adjusts instruction/facilitation to student/participant/client needs				
Comments:					

Domain D: Professionalism

Orientation to relationships and communities	Establishes effective relationships with colleagues/peers/faculty/students				
	Recognizes rights and responsibilities of others				
	Demonstrates effective communication				
	Demonstrates appropriate boundaries				
Enthusiasm and passion	Displays enthusiasm				
	Enjoys teaching/leading/facilitating				
Reflection	Reflects on tasks and teaching/leading/ facilitating				
	Responds to feedback				
Integrity	Acts in an ethical or moral manner				
	Values and exhibits honesty, personally and professionally				
Responsibility and work ethic	Arrives on time				
	Participates				
	Completes assigned tasks on schedule				
	Accepts personal responsibility				

Figure 6.4. *(continued)*

Commitment to professionalism	Sets high standards for professional behavior				
	Seeks professional development				
	Dresses in a professional manner/maintains hygiene				
Respect	Respects colleagues/peers/faculty/students				
	Listens to and values other opinions				
Comments:					

Figure 6.4. (continued)

dispositions assessment tool that may be filled out by each student's immediate supervisor or may also be used as a tool for self-assessment (see figure 6.4).

Minnesota State University@Mankato Experiential Education Master's Program: Assessment of Dispositions

Beginning January 2004, newly enrolled graduate students in the experiential education master's program at MSU will be asked to self-assess themselves according to the following four disposition domains upon entering the program and also toward the end of their final semester before graduating from the program. Additionally, the student's field supervisor will be asked to assess the student according to the following disposition domains during their practicum (ExEd 634) or internship (ExEd 635) field experience. (Field supervisors: Please mail or FAX a copy of the completed disposition survey to the student's advisor at Dept. of Educational Leadership, MSU, 115 Armstrong Hall, Mankato, MN, 56001, or FAX: 507-389-5863. It is also appropriate to provide the student with a copy of the completed survey.)

Student's name: _____

MSU advisor's name: _____

Month/year of entering master's in experiential education program: _____
Anticipated graduation, month/year: _____

Check one:
_____ Student Self-Assessment 1 (beginning of master's program)
_____ Student Self-Assessment 2 (near completion of master's program)
_____ Field Supervisor Assessment (near completion of internship or practicum experience)

If field supervisor assessment:
Name and title of supervisor: _____
Address: _____

_____
Phone: _____ E-mail: _____
Signature of student or field supervisor: _____
Today's date: _____

The four domains of this dispositions assessment tool—consisting of planning and preparation, learning environment, teaching for learning, and professionalism—are modeled after the work done by Charlotte Danielson (2002). She identified four domains of teaching that focus on specific skills teachers should strive to achieve. For instance, domain one (planning and preparation) is for the purpose of "organizing the content to engage students in learning" (p. 37). Engaging students in learning is a necessary skill in order to become an effective teacher.

At MSU, Mankato, the dispositions work group committee took these four domains and created an assessment tool for supervisors of student teachers. For consistency throughout the College of Education, faculty have taken this tool and adapted it for supervisors of experiential education graduate students. This comprehensive tool provides students with an assessment of their leadership skills, as well as their ability to teach. It gives supervisors, as well as graduate students using it as a self-assessment tool, specific information that differentiates four levels of proficiency, and when completed it provides students a clear understanding of their skill level.

Portfolios are the third form of assessment. At present, portfolios are not required in the program, but they are highly recommended and often compiled by students for optional credit. Many students complete portfolios to keep track of all their field-based experiences, and in the near future an academic course that covers portfolio development may be instituted for students in this program. Portfolios are an excellent way to track progress, from the beginning of the program to the end, and are also useful when highlighting related work experience and accomplishments to potential employers.

The contents of a portfolio will vary from student to student; however, key components are consistent for students in this program. The following are sample entries, in order, in a portfolio table of contents for experiential education students:

- Resume
- Statement of philosophy of education
- Learning contracts for project-based and field-based experiences
- Reflection papers for projects and field experiences
- Evaluations such as rubrics from classroom courses
- Evaluations such as dispositions forms from supervisors
- Self-assessment evaluations
- Teaching evaluations
- Abstract of thesis, alternate plan paper, or capstone project

All of these assessment tools help educators make important changes in the classroom, but they may also be useful in identifying potential programmatic changes as well. Once a year the experiential education graduate program completes an assessment plan that attempts to tie together learning outcomes for the entire program and helps instructors identify areas that may need improvement. The assessment plan also allows instructors to think about their long-range goals for their programs and provides a mechanism to track student progress during their academic programs. For instance, students in the experiential education program fill out a dispositions form at the beginning, middle, and end of their program so they can see how they have progressed over time.

The experiential education program assessment plan in figure 6.5 identifies different learning outcomes from the dispositions form, classroom

Student Learning Outcomes (performance, knowledge, attitudes)	Related College Goals	Related University Goals	Method(s) of Assessment	Who Assessed (students from what courses, population)	When Assessed (dates)	Standard of Mastery Criterion of Achievement	What Is Hoped to Be Learned?
1. Dispositions* in Planning and Preparation (for Field-Based Learning/Leading) Students will be able to:	1, 2, 5, 12, 14	1, 3, 4, 5, 6	Survey of Dispositions: Indirect Completed by students	Students entering exp. ed. master's program	During month of Sept. 2003 or Jan. 2004	100% of responses indicate disposition rating of "basic" or above	Identification of students' strengths and challenges in dispositions of planning and preparation
Demonstrate background knowledge Use appropriate approaches to planning	(Related Dept. Goals: 2)		Survey of Dispositions: Direct Completed by field supervisors	Students completing ExEd 634 Practicum or ExEd 635 Internship	During month of Dec. 2003 or April 2004	80% of responses indicate disposition rating of "satisfactory" or above	Identification of students' strengths and challenges in dispositions of planning and preparation
*outcomes include attitudes, knowledge, and skills			Survey of Dispositions: Indirect Completed by students	Students applying for graduation from program	During month of Dec. 2003 or April 2004	100% of responses indicate disposition rating of "satisfactory" or above	Identification of students' areas of improvement throughout program in dispositions of planning and preparation

Figure 6.5.   Assessment Plan Report Preparation Form for the Master's in Experiential Education Program, 2003–2004.
Source: JACarlson, 10/03/04.

2. Dispositions* in Learning Environment (for Field-Based Learning/Leading) Students will be able to:	1, 2, 5, 12, 14	1, 3, 4, 5, 6	Survey of Dispositions: Indirect Completed by students	Students entering exp. ed. master's program	During month of Sept. 2003 or Jan. 2004	100% of responses indicate disposition rating of "basic" or above	Identification of students' strengths and challenges in dispositions pertaining to learning environment
Foster a positive learning or work climate	(Related Dept. Goals: 2)		Survey of Dispositions: Direct Completed by field supervisors	Students completing ExEd 634 Practicum or ExEd 635 Internship	During month of Dec. 2003 or April 2004	80% of responses indicate disposition rating of "satisfactory" or above	Identification of students' strengths and challenges in dispositions pertaining to learning environment
*outcomes include attitudes, skills			Survey of Dispositions: Indirect Completed by students	Students applying for graduation from program	During month of Dec. 2003 or April 2004	100% of responses indicate disposition rating of "satisfactory" or above	Identification of students' areas of improvement throughout program in dispositions pertaining to learning environment
3. Dispositions* in Teaching for Learning (for Field-Based Learning/Leading) Students will be able to:	1, 2, 5, 12, 14	1, 3, 4, 5, 6	Survey of Dispositions: Indirect Completed by students	Students entering exp. ed. master's program	During month of Sept. 2003 or Jan. 2004	100% of responses indicate disposition rating of "basic" or above	Identification of students' strengths and challenges in dispositions pertaining to client/student learning
Use appropriate approaches to instruction	(Related Dept. Goals: 2)		Survey of Dispositions: Direct Completed by field supervisors	Students completing ExEd 634 Practicum or ExEd 635 Internship	During month of Dec. 2003 or April 2004	80% of responses indicate disposition rating of "satisfactory" or above	Identification of students' strengths and challenges in dispositions pertaining to client/student learning
*outcomes include attitudes, skills			Survey of Dispositions: Indirect Completed by students	Students applying for graduation from program	During month of Dec. 2003 or April 2004	100% of resp. indicate disp. rating of "satisfactory" or above	Identification of students' areas of improvement throughout program in dispositions pertaining to client/student learning

Figure 6.5. *(continued)*

Outcome	Dept. Goals	Standards	Assessment Method	Population	Timing	Criteria	Use of Results
4. Dispositions* in Professionalism Students will be able to: Build relationships Display enthusiasm and passion Engage in reflection Exhibit integrity Model responsible work ethic Interact respectfully	1, 2, 5, 12, 14	1, 3, 5	Survey of Dispositions: Indirect Completed by students	Students entering exp. ed. master's program	During month of Sept. 2003 or Jan. 2004	100% of responses indicate disposition rating of "basic" or above	Identification of students' strengths and challenges in dispositions of professionalism
			Survey of Dispositions: Direct Completed by field supervisors	Students completing ExEd 634 Practicum or ExEd 635 Internship	During month of Dec. 2003 or April 2004	80% of responses indicate disposition rating of "satisfactory" or above	Identification of students' strengths and challenges in dispositions of professionalism
*outcomes include attitudes, skills	(Related Dept. Goals: 2)		Survey of Dispositions: Indirect Completed by students	Students applying for graduation from program	During month of Dec. 2003 or April 2004	100% of responses indicate disposition rating of "satisfactory" or above	Identification of students' areas of improvement throughout program in dispositions of professionalism
5. Construction of Knowledge* Students will be able to: Demonstrate construction of knowledge through written expression Demonstrate construction of knowledge through oral expression	9, 12, 14	1, 2, 3, 5	Student Learning Logs: Direct Rubric evaluation by professor	Students in ExEd 645, Trends & Issues in Exp. Ed.	Each semester that course is offered	95% of responses reflect an understanding at level 3 or above	Identification of students' strengths and challenges, gains and growth in the construction of knowledge
			Student Presentations: Direct Rubric evaluation by professor	Students in ExEd 645, Trends & Issues in Exp. Ed.	Each semester that course is offered	95% of presentations reflect an understanding at level 3 or above	Identification of students' strengths and challenges, gains and growth in the construction of knowledge
*outcomes include knowledge, skills	(Related Dept. Goals: 2)		Student Presentations: Direct Rubric evaluation by professor	Students in ExEd 644, Philosophy of Exp. Ed.	Each semester that course is offered	95% of pres. reflect an understanding at level 3 or above	Identification of students' strengths and challenges, gains and growth in the construction of knowledge

Figure 6.5. (continued)

6. Disciplined Inquiry* in Project-Based Learning	9, 12, 14	1, 2, 3, 5	Student Reflective Evaluation Papers Learning Contracts: Direct Rubric evaluation by advisor or professor	Students in ExEd 603, Experience & Education, and ExEd 604, Development of Exp. Ed.	Throughout fall 2003 semester and spring 2004 semester	100% of papers reflect an understanding at level 3 or above	Identification of students' strengths and challenges, gains and growth in disciplined inquiry
Students will be able to:							
Synthesize the results and gains of their disciplined inquiry through written expression	(Related Dept. Goals: 2)		Student Projects: Direct Rubric evaluation by advisor or professor	Students in ExEd 603, Experience & Education, and ExEd 604, Development of Exp. Ed.	Throughout fall 2003 semester and spring 2004 semester	100% of projects reflect a quality at level 3 or above	Identification of students' strengths and challenges, gains and growth in disciplined inquiry
Synthesize the results and gains of their disciplined inquiry through project demonstration							
*outcomes include knowledge, skills, and attitudes							

* What will the department or program do with results of information?

1. Analyze feasibility and results of disposition survey. Make revisions to disposition survey or individual course curricula or other program dimensions accordingly, specifically in those areas where results fall below the level of "satisfactory" from field supervisors.

2. Continue monitoring the requirements and expectations of ExEd 644, ExEd 645, ExEd 603, and ExEd 604. Make revisions in course curricula or other program dimensions, specifically in those areas where rubric results fall below the level of 3 for either "understanding" or "quality."

* How did the department or program make use of the feedback from last year's assessment?

1. Feedback from last year's assessment was somewhat nebulous, resulting in an effort this year to more clearly assess the knowledge, skills, and attitudes (dispositions) gained by students in the experiential education program.

Figure 6.5. (*continued*)

courses, and project-based courses and ties them to college and university goals. Self-assessments, instructor assessments, and supervisor assessments are collected using rubrics, dispositions, learning contracts, and reflection papers. For instance, disposition outcomes for the four domains are collected from students and their supervisors via survey format; constructing knowledge in classroom courses is conducted by students and instructors using rubrics and self-assessment forms; and disciplined inquiry for projects is conducted by students and instructors using rubrics, learning contracts, and reflection papers.

At the end of the school year, an assessment report is completed and submitted. At MSU, Mankato, this is typically a short form that asks questions such as what learning outcomes were assessed, how were they assessed, what was learned from the assessment, and what changes will result from the assessment.

Assessment tools, plans, and reports do not have to be complicated or lengthy and should have one goal in mind—improving student learning. Most students prefer these tools over more traditional standards-based assessments because they allow them to assess their own learning, as well as provide them with an opportunity to discuss possible changes the educator might need to consider in order to promote a more effective learning environment. The key, however, to any assessment process is to generate discussion among faculty within a department on how to improve practices in the learning process, both in and out of the classroom.

BARRIERS TO OVERCOME

In 1998 the National Society for Experiential Education Foundations Document Committee published an article identifying the following as potential barriers that may prevent teachers from using experiential approaches in their classrooms: disorganization, chaos, time, and expense (www.nsee.org). There will always be barriers that impact the way educators teach their classes; however, some solutions may help minimize barriers such as these. Simply breaking the class into small groups may provide educators with more time, less chaos, and greater organization. Fullan (2001) suggests there are other, more challenging barriers to overcome. "Change in beliefs are even more difficult: they challenge the core values held by individuals regarding the purposes of education; moreover, beliefs are often not explicit, discussed, or understood, but rather are buried at the level of unstated assumptions" (p. 44). Challenging core values about education is necessary to change the predominant definition of knowledge from one that relies heavily on memorization to one that relies more on problem solving. When individuals change their core beliefs and become passionate about experiential learning, barriers begin to disappear.

I am fortunate that many students entering the experiential education graduate program at MSU, Mankato, do so because they are convinced that experiential learning is more effective than passive methods of learning. Some others, however, agree with the theory of experiential learning but argue that it cannot be implemented in the current education system. Networking, communication, and a little creativity may help these individuals overcome barriers that at first appeared insurmountable.

Committing oneself to using experiential learning in classroom settings is challenging and requires significant effort. Lecturing on how to dig a garden can be done in 50 minutes, but digging a garden may take the better part of a day. It requires work, but dividends can be enormous. Here are some of the barriers that teachers mention most often in my experiential education classes, along with a few ideas on how to overcome them.

ASSESSMENT

Classroom teachers in my courses often say something like, "I believe in the theory, but it's impossible to implement it in my classroom." When questioned further they usually cite assessment as the primary reason why they do not use experiential learning in their classes. The school calendar is tied to a series of standardized tests, and if students do not do well on these tests, schools—and even teachers—run the risk of having their names printed in their local newspapers for falling short on expected performance levels. Standards-based assessments promote the use of lecture because it is easier for students to do well on these tests if they are spoon-fed the necessary content, so teachers stay away from using experiential approaches to learning.

Most teachers that take my courses are convinced that experiential learning is more effective and results in higher order thinking skills than does the lecture format, but their hands are tied. Some teachers have even mentioned they use experiential learning at various times during the school year but convert back to lecturing and teaching to the test when necessary. This places teachers in an odd predicament because they know what works yet are forced to use an inferior teaching method. The best advice I have offered teachers in this situation is to continue using experiential learning whenever possible. In addition, teachers should share the *Breaking Ranks II* report (NASSP 2004) with their principals and point out how high school recommendations are focusing more on experiential learning and performance-based assessments rather than standards-based approaches.

CONTROL

The second most common barrier I hear from educators revolves around perception. Educators are concerned that others will perceive them as lacking control over their students or view them as being lazy if they allow students freedom to pursue their own interests. I understand this feeling because I continue to hear stories about the opposition who argue for stricter standards, less freedom, and more control in the classroom. When I give students freedom to work on projects and presentations during class, which means they are free to move about the class—or for that matter, the campus—to do research and collect resources, I discuss with students why I use this approach and prepare them for such arguments. One could perceive this approach as lacking content; however, for experiential learning to be effective, educators must give students freedom to pursue interests and learn how to take control of their own learning.

It is difficult to rid ourselves of past experiences from traditional education, where control, structure, and discipline were the norm. But, if educators want students to become self-directed learners, they must give them freedom to pursue their interests. Controlling students to do what educators want them to do makes them reliant, sometimes even unable to think for themselves. If freedom is abused, then educators must rein in the student and provide focus and direction. Educators should not fear this process, but instead be courageous and take a risk by allowing students freedom to become responsible learners.

TIME

A typical school day in traditional settings is broken up into a series of class periods usually ranging from 40 to 50 minutes in length. Unfortunately, activities, projects, and field experiences usually require longer blocks of time to complete. This leaves educators in traditional settings at a disadvantage from the very outset. Educators that begin to incorporate experiential learning become frustrated because of the lack of time, but short activities and projects can be incorporated in single class periods. In addition, educators can extend a single activity or project over several class periods, or even the entire length of the course.

I once had college students design a problem-solving curriculum for a high school math class where each activity could be accomplished within a 50-minute time frame. The high school students were actively engaged with their peers for the entire period. Educators can view numerous websites (see chapter five) to find activities and projects appropriate for their specific subject areas. Field experiences are usually more time consuming, and therefore more challenging to incorporate, but there are ways to include them in a semester-long course. In my undergraduate courses, I would often include field experiences as assignments that needed to be accomplished by the end of the semester. When I was teaching outdoor education courses, I would have students work with two or three professionals from different organizations to get a feel for the career opportunities in these fields. This often included weekend experiences, which were time consuming for students; however, they often mentioned that these experiences were the highlight of the course.

STUDENT NUMBERS

Another commonly mentioned barrier is large class size. Although it is easier to implement experiential learning with smaller numbers, it is still feasible with larger numbers as well. I have done workshops with 100 or more people in one- to three-hour time blocks using experiential learning. Time management in such situations is key. I begin by explaining the format so everyone knows what we are doing and where we are heading. I usually provide an overhead of the workshop or class format so that if students forget where they are in the process, a quick glance can help get them back on track. Once the large group is broken into groups of 10 to 15, educators can use experiential learning as if they had one small group.

With large groups, I typically use a combination of activities, projects, and group discussions where they discuss questions and report to the large group periodically. I may also ask them to create a plan or a project to implement once they return to their schools or organizations. Educators can use a similar format with large classes as well. Once groups are identified, educators can have students working together discussing various topics, engaging in different activities, and working on projects. They can even incorporate field experiences outside class time, which students can discuss in their small groups after completing them. As mentioned before, time management is critical, and it is important to facilitate the process by keeping students on task. Once educators determine the format for a given class, then it becomes a matter of explaining it to the class and facilitating the format. Obviously educators need to provide enough resources for all the small groups, so it may be a little more expensive to facilitate large groups depending upon the nature of the activities and resources needed.

SYSTEMIC PROBLEMS

One other barrier I have experienced several times, affecting universities more than high schools, focuses on bureaucratic policies. Schools and universities have created systems filled with bureaucracy. Allison and Zelikow (1999) suggest that the organizational behavior model, which relies heavily on bureaucratic policies and procedures to help organizations run smoothly, may backfire by actually slowing down progress (p. 143). One university I worked for created policies that rewarded the lecture format by assigning fewer workload hours to labs than to lectures. One-hour lectures received one hour of workload, whereas two-hour labs received only one hour of workload. This was a huge incentive for faculty members to teach lecture courses as opposed to labs, which tend to be more experiential in nature. When I first started teaching at this university, without realizing that labs held less value than lectures, I decided to change many of my courses to three-hour labs so I could incorporate more experiential learning opportunities. I filled out all the necessary curriculum forms and submitted them to the curriculum committee. Little did I know at the time that this policy was going to slow down progress in my attempts to create a more effective educator.

The curriculum committee responded to my proposal by saying I would either have to increase the number of lab hours per course or parcel up these courses to include a combination of lectures and labs to fulfill my workload. The system developed by the university was obviously not created with experiential educators in mind. I met with the curriculum committee several times over the year, trying to explain that learning did not result solely from a lecture or a lab. I suggested that learning was a combination of thinking and doing, and students need opportunities to leave the classroom and test out their ideas and theories in real-life situations. As an example, I mentioned a course I taught at another university where college students met at the local high school and taught various problem-solving and adventure activities to high school students. I explained to the committee that this course provided a wonderful opportunity for college students to experiment with teaching techniques and that I needed a full three hours for travel, preparation, discussion, teaching, and finally reflection. At one point in this discussion I told them to call it lecture or lab or whatever they wanted but that I needed a three-hour time block to do this course. It was an extremely challenging process, but in the end they decided to call it a three-hour lecture as long as I included some lecture in every class period. I agreed and the battle was over. In the end I realized that policies and procedures often create barriers for experiential educators, but if persistent, there are ways to mainstream experiential learning even within current traditional systems.

Other barriers exist as well, but these seem to be the ones teachers in my courses mention most often. During discussions about barriers, we often came to the conclusion that barriers are more perceived than real. Barriers can easily be created, preventing educators from implementing experiential learning, but for those individuals that are enthusiastic and dedicated to the process, barriers can be overcome.

REFERENCES

Airasian, P. W., & Abrams, L. M. (2002). What role will assessment play in school in the future? In R. W. Lissitz & W. D. Schafer (Eds.), *Assessment in Educational Reform*. Boston: Allyn & Bacon.

Allison, G., & Zelikow, P. (1999). *Essence of decision: Explaining the Cuban missile crisis*. New York: Addison Wesley.

Ball, D., & Cohen, D. (1999). Developing practice, developing practitioners: Towards a practice-based theory of professional education. In L. Darling-Hammond & G. Sykes (Eds.), *Teaching as the learning profession*. San Francisco: Jossey-Bass.

Boud, D., Cohen, R., & Walker, D. (1993). *Using experience for learning*. Bristol, PA: Open University Press.

Brookfield, S., & Preskill, S. (1999). *Discussion as a way of teaching*. San Francisco: Jossey-Bass.

Bruner, J. (1960). *The process of education*. Cambridge, MA: Harvard University Press.

Bunting, C., & Townley, J. (1999). A synthesis of environmental and adventure education concepts: a professional responsibility. In J. Miles & S. Priest (Eds.), *Adventure programming*. State College, PA: Venture Publishing.

Caine, G., & Caine, R. N. (2001). *The brain, education, and the competitive edge*. Lanham, MD: ScarecrowEducation.

Campbell, M. (1998). What is a learning expedition? In M. Campbell, M. Liebowitz, A. Mednick, & L. Rugen (Eds.), *Guide for planning a learning expedition*. Dubuque, IA: Kendall/Hunt.

Campbell, M. (1999). Introduction. In E. Cousins & A. Mednick (Eds.), *Service at the heart of learning: Teachers' writings*. Dubuque, IA: Kendall/Hunt.

Cohen, E. (1986). *Designing groupwork: Strategies for the heterogeneous classroom*. New York: Teachers College Press.

Coleman, J. (1976). Differences between experiential and classroom learning. In M. T. Keeton & Associates (Eds.), *Experiential learning*. San Francisco: Jossey-Bass.

Coleman, J. (1995). Experiential learning and information assimilation: Toward an appropriate mix. In K. Warren, M. Sakofs, & J. Hunt (Eds.), *The theory of experiential education*. Dubuque, IA: Kendall/Hunt.

Courts, P. L., & McInerny, K. H. (1993). *Assessment in higher education: Politics, pedagogy, and portfolios*. Westport, CT: Praeger.

Cousins, E., & Mednick, A. (1999). *Service at the heart of learning: Teachers' writings*. Dubuque, IA: Kendall/Hunt.

Danielson, C. (2002). *Enhancing student achievement: A framework for school improvement*. Alexandria, VA: Association for Supervision and Curriculum Development.

Dewey, J. (1916). *Democracy and education*. New York: Free Press.

Dewey, J. (1936). The theory of the Chicago experiment. In J. Boydston (Ed.), *The later works 1925–1953*. Vol II, p. 204. Carbondale, IL: Southern Illinois University Press.

Dewey, J. (1938). *Experience and education*. New York: Free Press.

Dewey, J. (1973). Experience and philosophic method and interest in relation to the training of the will. In J. J. McDermott (Ed.), *The philosophy of John Dewey*. University of Chicago Press.

Eyler, J., & Giles, D. E. (1999). *Where's the learning in service-learning?* San Francisco: Jossey-Bass.

Farrell, G. (1999). Foreword. In E. Cousins & A. Mednick (Eds.), *Service at the heart of learning: Teachers' writings*. Dubuque, IA: Kendall/Hunt.

Fink, L. D. (2003). *Creating significant learning experiences*. San Francisco: Jossey-Bass.

Fullan, M. (2001). *The new meaning of educational change* (3rd ed.). New York: Teachers College Press.

Gardner, H. (1991). *The unschooled mind: How children think and how schools should teach*. New York: Basic.

Gardner, H. (1993). *Frames of mind: The theory of multiple intelligence*. New York: Basic.

Heinecke, W. F., Curry-Corcoran, D. E., & Moon, T. R. (2003). U.S. schools and the new standards and accountability initiative. In D. Duke, M. Grogan, P. Tucker, & W. Heinecke (Eds.), *Educational leadership in an age of accountability*. Albany: State University of New York Press.

Henry, J. (1989). Meaning and practice in experiential learning. In S. Warner-Weil & I. McGill (Eds.), *Making sense of experiential learning: Diversity in theory and practice*. Bristol, PA: Open University Press.

Huberman, M. (1983). Recipes for busy kitchens. *Knowledge: Creation, Diffusion, Utilization, 4*, 478–510.

Hutchings, P., & Wutzdorff, A. (1988). Experiential learning across the curriculum: Assumptions and principles. In P. Hutchings and A. Wutzdorff (Eds.), *Knowing and doing: Learning through experience. New directions for teaching and learning*. San Francisco: Jossey-Bass.

Jacoby, B., & Associates. (1996). *Service learning in higher education*. San Francisco: Jossey-Bass.

Knoll, M. (1997). The project method: Its vocational education origin and international development. *Journal of Industrial Teacher Education, 34* (3), 59–80.

Lambert, L., Walker, D., Zimmerman, D. P., Cooper, J. E., Lambert, M. D., Gardner, M. E., & Szabo, M. (1995). *The constructivist leader*. New York: Teachers College Press.

Levine, A. (2002). *One kid at a time*. Columbia, NY: Teachers College Press.

Levine, A., & Cureton, J. S. (1998). *When hope and fear collide: A portrait of today's college student*. San Francisco: Jossey-Bass.

Martin-Kniep, G. O. (2000). *Becoming a better teacher: Eight innovations that work*. Alexandria, VA: Association for Supervision and Curriculum Development.

Marzano, R. J. (1992). *A different kind of classroom*. Alexandria, VA: Association for Supervision and Curriculum Development.

McKeachie, W. J. (1994). *Teaching tips: Strategies, research, and theory for college and university teachers*. Lexington, MA: D.C. Heath.

National Association of Secondary School Principals. (1996). *Breaking ranks: Changing an American institution*. A report of the National Association of Secondary School Principals in partnership with the Carnegie Foundation. Reston, VA: NASSP.

National Association of Secondary School Principals. (2004). *Breaking ranks II: Strategies for leading high school reform*. A report of the National Association of Secondary School Principals in partnership with the Education Alliance at Brown University. Reston, VA: NASSP.

National Society for Experiential Education Foundations Document Committee (1998). Foundations of experiential education, at www.nsee.org.

Newell, R. (2003). *Passion for learning*. Lanham, MD: ScarecrowEducation.

Newman, F., Secada, W., & Wehlage, G. (1995). *A guide to authentic instruction and assessment: Vision, standards, and scoring*. Madison, WI: Wisconsin Center for Education Research.

Pollio, H. R. (1984). What students think about and do in college lecture courses. *Teaching Learning Issues, 53*.

Reeves, D. B. (2004). *Accountability for learning: How teachers and school leaders can take charge*. Alexandria, VA: Association for Supervision and Curriculum Development.

Rhoades, R., & Howard, J. P. F. (1998). *Academic service learning: A pedagogy of action and reflection*. San Francisco, CA: Jossey-Bass.

Roeber, E. D. (2002). How will we gather the data we need to inform policy makers? In R. W. Lissitz & W. D. Schafer (Eds.), *Assessment in educational reform*. Boston, MA: Allyn & Bacon.

Rothman, R. (2001). One hundred fifty years of testing. In *The Jossey-Bass Reader on School Reform*. San Francisco: Jossey-Bass.

Secretary's Commission on Achieving Necessary Skills, U.S. Department of Labor. (2001). Learning a living: A blueprint for high performance. SCANS report for America 2000 executive summary principles and recommendations. In *The Jossey-Bass Reader on School Reform*. San Francisco: Jossey-Bass.

Serow, R. (1998). *Program evaluation handbook*. Needham Heights, MA: Simon & Schuster Custom Publishing.

Silva, P., & Mackin, R. A. (2002). *Standards of mind and heart: Creating the good high school*. New York: Teachers College Press.

Sizer, T. (1984). *Horace's compromise: The dilemma of the American high school*. Boston: Houghton Mifflin.

Sizer, T. (1992). *Horace's school: Redesigning the American high school*. Boston: Houghton Mifflin.

Stanton, T., Giles D. E., & Cruz, N. I. (1999). *Service learning: A movement's pioneers reflect on its origins, practice, and future*. San Francisco: Jossey-Bass.

Starnes, B. A. (1999). *The Foxfire approach to teaching and learning: John Dewey, experiential learning, and the core practices*. Charleston, WV: Clearinghouse on Rural Education and Small Schools.

Stiggins, R. J. (2002). Where is our assessment future and how can we get there from here? In R. W. Lissitz & W. D. Schafer (Eds.), *Assessment in educational reform*. Boston: Allyn & Bacon.

Van Til, W. (1969). *The laboratory school: Its rise and fall*. Eric Document 034703.

Wald, P. J., & Castleberry, M. S. (2000). *Educators as learners: Creating professional learning communities*. Alexandria, VA: Association for Supervision and Curriculum Development.

Warner-Weil, S., & McGill, I. (1989). *Making sense of experiential learning: Diversity in theory and practice*. Bristol, PA: Open University Press.

Whitehead, A. N. (1929). *The aims of education*. New York: Free Press.

Wiggens, G. (1998). *Educative assessment: Designing assessments to inform and improve student performance*. San Francisco: Jossey-Bass.

Wurdinger, S., & Priest, S. (1999). Integrating theory and application in experiential learning. In J. Miles & S. Priest (Eds.), *Adventure Programming*. State College, PA: Venture.

www.aee.org/ndef/html

www.buyindies.com/listings/8/7/AIMS-8728.html

www.education.state.mn.us/html/intro_data_student_data.htm

www.marssociety.org/MDRS/team/msupport.asp

www.newsobserver.com/features/sundayjournal/story/3560466p-3163354c.html

www.nsee.org

www.nysut.org/newyorkteacher/2002-2003/030129history.html

www.wested.org/pblnet/exemplary_projects.html

ABOUT THE AUTHOR

Scott D. Wurdinger is a professor of experiential education and leadership studies and coordinator of the experiential education graduate program at Minnesota State University in Mankato, Minnesota. He is author of *Philosophical Issues in Adventure Education* and coauthor of *Controversial Issues in Adventure Education* and *Developing Challenge Course Programs for Schools*. He lives in Mankato with his wife, Annette, and daughters, Madeline and Lauren.

Made in the USA
San Bernardino, CA
14 December 2016